TWO REMINISCENCES
OF
THOMAS CARLYLE

TWO REMINISCENCES

OF

THOMAS CARLYLE

Now First Published

Edited by

JOHN CLUBBE

DUKE UNIVERSITY PRESS
Durham, N.C.
1974

© 1974, Duke University Press

L.C.C. card no. 73–81497

I.S.B.N. 0–8223–0307–8

PRINTED IN THE UNITED
STATES OF AMERICA

For

DOROTHY ELAINE ROBERTS

Contents

Preface

In the summer of 1969 I went to Scotland to work in the extraordinary collection of Carlyle's papers housed in the National Library in Edinburgh. The year before I had begun preparing a one-volume abridgment and revision of James Anthony Froude's great four-volume Victorian life of Carlyle. Since its publication early in the 1880's, Froude's life has come under severe attack for its inaccurate and sometimes misleading quotations from Carlyle's correspondence, and one of my tasks was to correct his texts against the originals. Many of the letters which Froude used I had already consulted through xeroxes in the research files at Duke assembled by my colleague Charles Richard Sanders for the ongoing collected edition of the Carlyles' correspondence. But several crucial texts still eluded my grasp. One in particular I hoped very much to find: the account, from which Froude quoted passages in his first volume, in which Carlyle made extensive and highly significant comments on *Sartor Resartus*. Froude never gave his source for these quotations, and my only clue was a tantalizing footnote "alluding to a German biography in which he [Carlyle] was said to have learnt Hebrew." With this in mind, early in my work at the National Library I called for MS 1799, described in the catalogue as "Remarks by Carlyle, 1866, on Friedrich Althaus's article 'Thomas Carlyle, Eine biographisch-literarische Charakteristik,' in *Unsere Zeit*, 1 July 1866." A moment's skimming told me I had found what I wanted.

Oddly enough, Froude never mentioned Althaus by name. Further investigation revealed that he had quoted only a few passages from a much longer manuscript. After he had written his first volume, he virtually ignored Carlyle's notes and Althaus's biography—a biography Carlyle called the best yet written of him—and, with few exceptions, writers on Carlyle since Froude's day have ignored both. What emerged from further examination of the manuscript was the care with which Carlyle had keyed his comments to Althaus's narrative. For one to grasp the full implications of each they must be read together. Again, Froude gave no hint of this complementary relationship.

I had found, in effect, a new reminiscence by Carlyle, largely on himself and his career, written at the same time he was writing his other reminiscences, and consciously designed by him to supplement them. In it, he speaks of his schooling and university career, of his plans for the ministry, of Professor John Leslie and of his relationship with Edward Irving, of the gradual working out at Hoddam Hill in 1825–1826 of his 1822 conversion, of his possible emigration to America in the 1830's, and of his father and mother and brother Alexander. He leaves valuable statements on the extent of his acquaintance with classical literatures and on his first knowledge of German, on other works beside *Sartor* (especially the *Life of Schiller*, *German Romance*, and *Frederick the Great*), on his intellectual debts to Goethe and to Jean Paul, on the development of his singular literary style, and on the "might is right" maxim popularly attributed to him. His clarifying comments on a host of other points, biographical and critical, will require significant modifications in subsequent accounts of his achievement.

Before proceeding further with my work on Froude, I decided that the Althaus biography with Carlyle's notes was of sufficient importance to merit publication in its own right, and to facilitate use of the biography by scholars who do not know German I thought it best to translate it. A few days after my discovery, I came across another unpublished reminiscence by Carlyle in the National Library. Much briefer than the Althaus, it memorializes Adam Skirving and his son, the eccentric painter Archibald, who had befriended the young Jane Welsh. Carlyle's graphic pen portrait of the younger Skirving ranks among his best. The appearance in print of both narratives completes the publication of Carlyle's reminiscences.

Preparing an edition of unpublished manuscripts leaves one with a keen sense of one's debts to others. Even though a long list of helpers may seem disproportionate for so short a book, I wish to thank here the always genial members of the reference staff of the Duke·University Library; J. Emerson Ford, Director of the Interlibrary Loan Service; several of my colleagues in the English Department, chiefly Oliver W. Ferguson, and Robert Krueger; Peter H. Burian of the Classics Department, for aid with Carlyle's classical allusions; Leland R. Phelps,

PREFACE

for similar help with German allusions; Judith Barnes, for her finely-developed sense of style and for much else; Susan A. Boughton, for a careful reading of the manuscript; and Dorothy Roberts, for encouragement in more ways than I can hope to thank her for, not least of which was the typing of the manuscript with her usual expertise. I owe a particular debt to Rowland E. Cross for taking time from an unusually busy schedule to read my English translation of the Althaus biography. Every page bears the stamp of his valuable criticism. In the preparation of the Skirving reminiscence, I acknowledge with gratitude the help of Richard Johnson, Basil Skinner of the University of Edinburgh, A. M. Mackensie of the Scottish National Portrait Gallery, and Mrs. Leila Hoskins of Cheltenham, England, a descendant of Adam Skirving. Both official readers of my manuscript went over it with care and made many useful suggestions, as did Ian Campbell of the University of Edinburgh and Charles Richard Sanders of Duke. My debt to Professor Sanders extends further, in that he has generously allowed me to use the files of Carlyle's letters which he has built up over the years. Without this aid my progress would have been greatly slowed if not stopped.

I wish to acknowledge the permission of the Trustees of the National Library of Scotland to publish the two reminiscences and, in particular, the help kindly given me by James S. Ritchie, Deputy Keeper of the Department of Manuscripts. I am grateful to the Duke University Press for allowing me to pilfer several notes from the first four volumes of *The Collected Letters of Thomas and Jane Welsh Carlyle* and to the University's Council on Research for its steady support of my work and for awarding this volume a publication subvention.

J. C.

Duke University
Durham, N.C.

Abbreviations and Short Titles

Althaus (1869) Althaus, Friedrich. "Thomas Carlyle." *Englische Charakterbilder*, 2 vols. (Berlin: Verlag der Königlichen Geheimen Ober-Hofbuchdruckerei [R. v. Decker], 1869), I, 235–322 (a slightly revised version of the biography of Carlyle first published in *Unsere Zeit* in 1866)

Althaus, "Erinnerungen" Althaus, Friedrich. "Erinnerungen an Thomas Carlyle" [Recollections of Thomas Carlyle]. *Unsere Zeit*, I [n.s.] (June 1881), 824–852

CL Carlyle, Thomas. *The Collected Letters of Thomas and Jane Welsh Carlyle. 1812–1828*. Duke-Edinburgh Edition. Ed. Charles Richard Sanders, Kenneth J. Fielding, Ian M. Campbell, John Clubbe, and Janetta Taylor. 4 vols. Durham, North Carolina: Duke University Press, 1970

DNB *Dictionary of National Biography*

Dyer Dyer, I. W. *A Bibliography of Thomas Carlyle's Writings and Ana*. Portland, Maine: Southworth Press, 1928

Froude, *Carlyle* Froude, J. A. *Thomas Carlyle: A History of the First Forty Years of His Life, 1795–1835; A History of His Life in London, 1834–1881*. 4 vols. London: Longmans, Green, 1882; 1884

Harrold, *CGT* Harrold, Charles Frederick. *Carlyle and German Thought: 1819–1834*. New Haven: Yale University Press, 1934

Harrold, *Sartor* Harrold, Charles Frederick, ed. *Sartor Resartus*. New York: Odyssey Press, 1937

JAC John Aitken Carlyle (1801–1879), brother of Thomas Carlyle

JWC Jane Welsh Carlyle (1801–1866), wife of Thomas Carlyle

LL Carlyle, Alexander, ed. *The Love Letters of Thomas Carlyle and Jane Welsh.* 2 vols. London and New York: John Lane, 1909

Marrs Marrs, Edwin W., Jr., ed. *The Letters of Thomas Carlyle to His Brother Alexander, With Related Family Letters.* Cambridge, Mass.: Harvard University Press, 1968

NLS National Library of Scotland, Edinburgh

Norton, *GC* Norton, Charles Eliot, ed. *Correspondence between Goethe and Carlyle.* London and New York: Macmillan, 1887

Norton, *L26–36* Norton, Charles Eliot, ed. *Letters of Thomas Carlyle, 1826–1836.* London and New York: Macmillan, 1889

Reminiscences Carlyle, Thomas. *Reminiscences.* Ed. C. E. Norton. 2 vols. London and New York: Macmillan, 1887

Slater, *CEC* Slater, Joseph, ed. *The Correspondence of Emerson and Carlyle.* New York and London: Columbia University Press, 1964

TC Thomas Carlyle (1795–1881)

Tennyson, *Sartor* Tennyson, G. B. *Sartor Called Resartus. The Genesis, Structure, and Style of Thomas Carlyle's First Major Work.* Princeton, N.J.: Princeton University Press, 1965

Wilson, *Carlyle* Wilson, David Alec. *Carlyle.* 6 vols. London: Kegan Paul, Trench, Trubner and Co., Ltd.; New York: E. P. Dutton and Co., 1923–1934

Works Carlyle, Thomas. *Works.* Centenary Edition. Ed. H. D. Traill. 30 vols. London: Chapman and Hall, 1896–1899

THOMAS CARLYLE

A Biographical and Literary Portrait

by

FRIEDRICH ALTHAUS

Translated from the German

with

THOMAS CARLYLE'S NOTES

Editor's Introduction

In 1866 Carlyle stood at the pinnacle of his fame. The year before, Chapman and Hall had published the final two volumes of the six-volume *History of Frederick the Great*, the titanic work many of Carlyle's contemporaries judged his greatest achievement as a historian. That same year the students at the University of Edinburgh elected him their Rector. On 2 April of the year following he delivered his inaugural address, which John Tyndall described to Jane Welsh Carlyle as "a perfect triumph!"[1] It was indeed, and Carlyle, tarrying among his Scottish relatives, savored it to the full. But not three weeks after, on 19 April, his wife of forty years died suddenly—and his triumph turned to ashes. The distraught husband hastened back to the now desolate house at 5 Cheyne Row, there to plunge into a profound gloom and remorse that ended only with his life in 1881. These two events, the one "proud and happy" and the other "sorrowful,"[2] were still fresh in the public mind when the editor of the German periodical *Unsere Zeit* asked Friedrich Althaus to write "a general overview of Carlyle's life and literary activity."[3] In an article "Erinnerungen an Thomas Carlyle," published in the spring of 1881 shortly after Carlyle's death, Althaus relates how he came to write the "overview" or biography and to know Carlyle. This story forms an interesting but relatively little-known episode in the immensely well-documented life of the Sage of Chelsea.

Long familiar with Carlyle's major writings, Althaus willingly accepted the assignment to write a biography of him. "As a literary figure and a national influence," he wrote in his "Recollections" of 1881, he considered Carlyle "the Samuel Johnson of the nineteenth century." To him, Carlyle was "a great prose poet"; he was "without question" the

1. *Letters and Memorials of Jane Welsh Carlyle*, ed. James Anthony Froude (London: Longmans, 1883), III, 318.
2. Althaus's words in his biography.
3. Althaus, "Erinnerungen," p. 825. Subsequent quotations from this source are identified by page numbers within the text. All translations are mine.

3

greatest essayist and historian England had brought forth. But although he had in his lifetime aroused "greater personal interest than anyone since Lord Byron" (p. 824), finding accurate biographical information about him proved extraordinarily difficult. "I soon fell into no slight dilemma," Althaus recalled in 1881.

> There was no lack of biographical notices and scattered facts, yet all in all these were extremely unsatisfactory; especially for the beginnings of his career were the dates full of gaps. Finally I had to turn to Carlyle himself with a series of questions, but in this received no reply. The outlook for my work thus seemed very discouraging. Not yet wishing to abandon my efforts in this negative result, I encountered soon afterwards a Scots friend to whom I complained of my problem. He did not know Carlyle himself, but he knew a German countryman who, as he informed me, had known Carlyle for years and from whom I, in any case, would be able to learn more about him than from any other source. This was Neuberg, the translator of the *History of Frederick the Great*, and who lived quite near me in London. At my request, my Scots friend told this German friend of Carlyle's of my wishes, and a few days later I received an invitation from Neuberg to visit him. (p. 826)

Joseph Neuberg, who had served for over fifteen years as Carlyle's amanuensis and literary assistant, greeted Althaus warmly. The two men soon found themselves in animated conversation about Carlyle. "One question led to another," Althaus continues.

> Neuberg could enlighten me immediately on many doubtful points; on others he too was uncertain, but kindly and readily promised to make inquiries of Carlyle himself. At Neuberg's instigation, Carlyle now told him much about his life, which he thus repeated to me, the greater part in Carlyle's very words. Under these circumstances we saw each other often. (ibid.)

Over the years Neuberg had proven his qualities of diligence and reliability as much as he had his complete integrity. His memory of minutiae, his faithfulness to fact, his care, his honesty—above all, his devotion to Carlyle—made him ideally suited to carry back to Althaus full and accurate information. For Althaus, it was a stroke of incredibly good

4

fortune to stumble upon him and to have him agree to serve as inter-
mediary between himself and Carlyle.[4]

Quite understandably, Althaus still made a few factual mistakes.
Either Carlyle had been elusive or vague or unclear, or Neuberg had
misunderstood him, or Althaus had misunderstood Neuberg. The
possibilities for error were considerable. Furthermore, as Althaus pointed
out in 1881, Neuberg and he were "on many points, even in respect to
Carlyle, of differing opinions" (p. 830). Probably he refers to his interpre-
tations of Carlyle's works, which he would have viewed from a liberal
stance and thus more critically than the conservative, hero-worshipping
Neuberg, but he may also have disagreed with him about the significance
of events in Carlyle's life. Neuberg was nonetheless pleased by the sketch.
"Even Carlyle himself," Althaus wrote in 1881, "wrote me a friendly
letter of acknowledgment" (ibid.). At this time he would gladly have
made Carlyle's acquaintance, but, knowing of Carlyle's despondency, he
was too shy to mention his desire, even to Neuberg himself.

In the weeks following his bereavement, Carlyle had remained to
himself, writing to no one, seeing no one but his brother John and
Margaret Welsh. A letter of 1 May to his old friend Thomas Erskine
best describes his state of mind and what he proposed to do:

> Indeed, I find it is best when I do not even speak to anybody. The
> stroke that has fallen on me is immeasurable, and has shattered in
> pieces my whole existence, which now suddenly lies all in ruins round
> me. In her name, whom I have lost, I must try to repair it, rebuild
> it into something of order for the few years or days that may remain
> to me, try not to waste them further, but to do something useful with
> them, under the stern monition I have had. If I but can, that should
> be my way of honouring her, whose history on earth now lies before
> me, all bathed in sorrow, but beautiful exceedingly, nay, of a kind of
> epic grandeur and heroic nobleness, known only to one heart now.[5]

A death in his immediate family always moved Carlyle intensely. Forced
to think through his own life in relation to the person now dead, he
gained relief from the great mental stress he underwent through expressing
his emotion in a prose as heartfelt and sad as it was objective. This he had

---

4. See Althaus, "Erinnerungen," pp. 826–830. Carlyle and Althaus discussed which
one of them was to write a memoir of Neuberg, but in the end neither did.
5. Froude, *Carlyle*, IV, 317–318.

done after the death of his favorite sister Margaret in 1830, after that of his father in 1832, and after that of his mother in 1853. Although only the unexpected death of his father while Carlyle was in London called forth from him an extended reminiscence, he evoked in letters at the time and throughout his life the memories of Margaret and his mother. Jane's sudden death, again while he was away, was the most tremendous blow of all. "He had scarcely slept . . . since the funeral," Froude wrote of Carlyle early in May. "He could not 'cry.' He was stunned and stupefied. He had never realised the possibility of losing her. He had settled that he would die first, and now she was gone."[6]

During these weeks, believing his own death near and not wishing to remain idle, Carlyle began to sift through his wife's letters and journals. Long-buried memories of his past life with her awoke in him, and he was moved to write a brief account of her last months. A mutual acquaintance had asked Geraldine Jewsbury, long a friend of both Carlyles, to put on paper her recollections and anecdotes of Mrs. Carlyle. Carlyle read the notes she prepared for him and was prompted, beginning on 25 May, to correct them and then to supplement them with a narrative of his own. Each morning he worked steadily on this reminiscence of Jane, speaking to no one of what he was doing and finishing his task on 28 July. Two days afterwards, he described his mood to his nephew James Carlyle as "not miserable; but I have to define it as very *wae* nearly always; sad altogether & serious altogether,—as well behoves in these new circumstances that have come."[7] Man's chief salvation on earth was work, Carlyle had often said, and not until now did he grasp the full dimensions of this terrible truth for himself.

Sometime in July he had received, probably from the author himself, Althaus's biography. Recognizing its importance, he thought "of having the poor Piece *interleaved* . . . and of perhaps correcting one or two blunders here & there."[8] In mid-August he took it with him to Ripple Court, near Dover, the residence of his old friend Miss Davenport Bromley, but he found the quiet comfort of Ripple Court too great for the intellectual and, for him, excruciating labor of reminiscing over his past life. Consequently, it was not until after his return to London at the end of

6. Ibid., pp. 322–323.
7. Letter in the possession of Mrs. E. M. Davidson.
8. Carlyle's preface to the Althaus biography. Subsequent quotations from Carlyle's notes to Althaus are not footnoted.

August that he sat down and wrote his comments—some a few words, others the length of several paragraphs—in the margins or inserted leaves of the Althaus biography. Despite his referring to it as a "poor Piece," Carlyle viewed it with unusual regard: "this," he said, "on the whole, is considerably the best Sketch I have seen on the subject." No greater praise could come from one who had long advocated high and demanding standards for the art of biography. With much pain and yet with some small satisfaction, he finished his commentary on 10 September and bound it up with Althaus's narrative. Although he professed indifference to the fate of both, he laid them carefully away with his other personal papers.

The man who wrote this "best Sketch" of Carlyle was born on 14 May 1829 in Detmold, a town in the idyllic Weser valley in agricultural north-central Germany. His father, for whom he was named and whose third son he was, was general superintendent of Lippe-Detmold, "a Protestant dignity" which, according to the *DNB*, is "equivalent to the Anglican rural dean." Theodor, the eldest son, born in 1822, led until his early death at the age of thirty an intense existence as a political activist and writer. An idealistic democrat, he fervidly supported the revolutionary movement of 1848 and after its failure landed in prison. *Aus dem Gefängnis* (1850), which tells of his experiences there, has earned him a more lasting fame than that which Friedrich achieved despite his more voluminous writings and the respected public position he attained. Friedrich commemorated his brother in *Theodor Althaus: Ein Lebensbild*, published in 1888. Never as politically radical, he must yet have gained from his brother's experience full and painful awareness of the con-temporary German political scene. His decision to leave Germany some-time after 1852 (probably soon after, for Carlyle in 1866 describes him as having long resided in England) may in part be attributable to discomfort within a country that had become increasingly conservative after the failure of the 1848 revolution. A younger brother, Julius, also emigrated to England, where he achieved sufficient distinction in medicine to warrant inclusion in the *DNB Supplement*.

Like many young Germans of his class, Althaus attended the university, in his case Bonn and Leipzig, and in 1852 he received his doctorate from Berlin with a dissertation, *De historiae conscriptionis historia* (*The History of the Writing of History*). Although he takes up only the Greek and Roman historians, his interest in historiography suggests the appeal which

Carlyle's writings would later hold for him. After he came to England, he earned his living, as Carlyle notes, by writing on English subjects for German journals and by schoolteaching. At the time he wrote the biography of Carlyle he was a regular correspondent for *Unsere Zeit* and taught German at Woolwich Military Academy outside London. In 1866 he lived at 4 Winchester Road, St. John's Wood, in London.

The 1860's must have been a decade of intense intellectual effort for Althaus. The knowledge evident in the more than eleven hundred pages of his two-volume *Englische Charakterbilder*, published in 1869, amply demonstrates that he had made a thorough study of contemporary English history and culture. In the preface, he states that England's insular position had conditioned the special nature of her irregular, individual development; furthermore, her reserved national character increased the difficulty for anyone trying to fathom her essential qualities. Although fully cognizant of the tremendous changes which English society had undergone during the preceding fifteen years, he refused to credit those who predicted irresistible decline for England. Rather, he accurately foresaw "a great period of reform legislation and national rebirth." The biographies published in the volumes had appeared earlier in the pages of *Unsere Zeit*. His subjects span the political spectrum and include Disraeli (which Carlyle thought the best), Palmerston and Cobden; Carlyle and Thackeray represent the humanities; Mill, philosophy; Turner, painting. Several of them Althaus may have chosen for the interest their careers aroused in Germany. He also included chapters on Ireland, reform, the Isle of Wight, cricket and hunting. Probably Althaus's most important book, *Englische Charakterbilder* can be read even today as one of the shrewder foreign analyses of Victorian England.

Though he wrote less in the remaining decades of his life, Althaus continued to publish in German periodicals biographies of important Englishmen—among them, "Lord Brougham" (1869), "Charles Dickens" (1871), "Charles James Fox" (1876), "Lord John Russell" (1879). In between, he translated into German Forster's *Life of Dickens*. He resigned his position at Woolwich Academy in 1874 to accept an appointment as professor of German at University College, London, then very much a struggling institution. This position he held, apparently without great distinction, for twenty-three years until his death in 1897.

Of Althaus's personal life we know almost nothing. He was married by the time he wrote the biography of Carlyle, for Carlyle speaks of him as "a perfectly respectable and quietly diligent Householder & Pater-familias among us." He had at least one son, Theodor Friedrich. A score of letters and notes must have passed between Althaus and Carlyle, but probably none of them are of great significance since Althaus, once he became acquainted with Carlyle, preferred to discuss more important matters with him in conversation. Almost none of this correspondence has been found, and efforts to trace the family have proved unavailing. In person, Althaus "was a big man, and ponderous, slow of speech and movement"[9]— qualities reflected in the measured pace and careful proportions of his Carlyle biography. Together with his journalist's interest in the revealing detail, they made him, as D. A. Wilson has said, "a faithful observer and trustworthy reporter."[10] From the pages of his biography, he emerges as a man of intellectual discernment and of liberal and humane principle.

Neuberg's sister, with Carlyle's permission, selected Althaus to complete the German translation of *Frederick*. When he died in March 1867 Neuberg had done about half the fifth volume, and it fell to Althaus to finish it and translate the sixth. Questions in regard to the work soon arose in his mind. After requesting an interview with Carlyle, he called for the first time at Cheyne Row on 16 October 1867. In his "Recollections" of Carlyle published in 1881, he describes graphically the appearance of the man whose biography he had written. Wilson has made some use of these descriptions; otherwise, English-speaking students of Carlyle have ignored them. Althaus found Carlyle otherwise than he had expected:

> His words, spoken quickly and in an undertone as if to himself, flowed on in an uninterrupted stream and allowed me only to half-comprehend many other remarks. I had imagined him different in this respect: more sparing of words, more forceful, speaking with a more marked emphasis. His appearance also corresponded only in part to the image I had formed from stories and photographs. He appeared to me tall but not haggard, and his slightly bowed bearing did not accord with my idea of the gruff acerbity of his character. I had imagined the head more massive, the brow (which was more broad than high) not so covered with thick gray hair, the face not so emaciated by his bushy, still half-gray beard. His eagle nose also surprised me, and in the glance of his blue-gray eyes I was struck

9. F. T. Frankau, nephew of Neuberg, in Wilson, *Carlyle*, VI, 143.
10. Ibid.

more by a lightning quickness and penetration than by a deep resigned melancholy. But even his friends had found him greatly changed after the death of his wife, still more after his return from Italy, and my imaginary portrait of him came from an earlier time. (p. 833)

When Carlyle offered to accompany him part of the way back to St. John's Wood, Althaus put the finishing touches on his portrait:

In his long black coat hanging below his knees, his broad folded linen collar set over his old-fashioned high stiff black necktie, and his gaiters, his appearance reminded me of a German professor, and if I were to meet him without knowing who it was I would have taken him for one. (pp. 833–834)

Althaus visited Carlyle in January 1869 and again in March after he had finished the translation of *Frederick*. "It seemed," he wrote of this latter visit,

as if I had never seen before so bushy, so venerable a head: the thick gray hair hung low over his forehead, the beard was brushed toward the face, the eyebrows fell thickly over the deep-set gray eyes. Later, he took a comb from his pocket and combed his hair all the way toward the front and then back against his brow; but the bushy gray setting of the weather-tanned face impressed me as characteristic. Within, it seemed to me, lay something solitary, withdrawn from the world, veiled. I often wished that he would throw off this shock of hair completely and let his face freely emerge: only then would he be seen as he is. (p. 838)

The Carlyle whom Althaus describes in *Unsere Zeit* in 1866 is the Carlyle whom Julia Margaret Cameron photographed with such great sensitivity soon afterwards. Her photographs, Rembrandtian in their play of light and shade, capture the *wae* state of mind that now marked Carlyle's life. "Terrifically ugly and woe-begone, but has something of likeness: my candid opinion," Carlyle said of these photographs.[11] No representation of him at this time is more faithful to his features and to his mood than the one reproduced in this volume.

In their meetings, Althaus questioned Carlyle about English turns of phrase in *Frederick* which he could not translate—expressions such as

11. Anne Thackeray Ritchie, *Alfred, Lord Tennyson and His Friends* (London: T. Fisher Unwin, 1893), p. 12.

"the Horn-gate of Dreams," the "deciduous gardenings of Sans-Souci, better than any Rialto at its best," "ye melodious torrents of Gadarene swine," and "a tragic zany." It should not be held against him if occasionally he falters in decoding Carlyle's metaphorical splendor, for his competence as a translator is considerable. Carlyle gladly gave him the assistance he needed. Althaus's last description of him seizes his manner of utterance:

> Carlyle was in a most amiable mood. The tone and style of his conversation gave me exactly the same impression as did the reading of his books. He generally spoke in this way whenever I saw him, and of course with the greatest liveliness and naturalness. For my part, I never noticed in him—despite all the vigor with which he expressed his opinions—a trace of the dogmatic tone which others have mentioned as disturbing. If his talk occasionally took on the form of a monologue carried on in an undertone, still he was equally ready to listen and to answer. (pp. 841–842)

In the years that followed, the two men, living far apart in London, met at more infrequent intervals. Mutual respect characterized their relationship to the last. During the Franco-Prussian War, Althaus tried to enlist Carlyle's backing for Germany's annexation of Alsace and Lorraine. Although he failed in his mission, it was, as he said, only an apparent failure, for on 18 November 1870 appeared Carlyle's famous letter in *The Times* in support of Germany's aims. The two men met for the last time at the end of July 1877. They spoke of the past, of the success of the People's Edition of Carlyle's *Works* (especially of *Sartor*'s continued appeal), and of Goethe. The conversation continued in a long walk and bus ride, after which they parted. Not once in any of their meetings had Carlyle mentioned either Althaus's biography of himself or the extensive notes which he had made to it when it first appeared in *Unsere Zeit* in 1866. "All the more surprising was it to me now," Althaus wrote after Carlyle's death in 1881, "as I found out recently, that my work had been of real interest to him in that sad time." From Carlyle's old friend Max Müller he learned "that a copy of my essay with detailed comments in his own hand was among his literary remains, and I need not say with what feelings I read these pages which Mr. Froude, Carlyle's literary executor, had the kindness to pass on to me" (p. 830).

Althaus bases his biography on extensive knowledge and wide curiosity;

throughout, he is friendly and fair-minded to Carlyle. His setting of Carlyle's thought within the perspective of English history and civilization is manifest throughout the biography and is perhaps its chief strength. His wide studies in the humanities and in history, his thorough familiarity with the English scene, his honesty and objectivity are all evident in it and would have been valued by Carlyle. His biography reveals a philosophical mind at work interpreting the life of its subject as it unfolds. The care of its research and the artistic shaping of its material allows it to transcend its journalistic origins. Typically, Althaus refused to be satisfied by the limited information he found in published biographical sketches and sought firsthand knowledge. Though he probably values Carlyle's achievement more highly than would a biographer today, he does not hesitate to disagree with him when he thinks he is unfair. Even his disagreements serve a useful purpose, as, for example, when his interpretation of the "Rights and Mights" chapter of *Chartism* called forth from Carlyle a significant clarifying statement. Carlyle's comments usually confirm the authenticity of Althaus's account; often they add to it. Basing his narrative on the "very words" which Neuberg brought back from Carlyle, Althaus could make it, in its critical as well as in its biographical sections, far superior to anything which had appeared before. Although necessarily outdated in many places, it still has biographical information found nowhere else and is often persuasive critically. In remaining one of the sounder short biographies of Carlyle, it reminds us once again that much of the best that has been said of the Victorians they said themselves.

No one will ever determine which passages of Althaus's life are based on Carlyle's "very words." Each student of Carlyle must sift it for himself. Certain information seems authentically firsthand in that it had not appeared elsewhere prior to Althaus and could have come only from Carlyle himself. Such would be the paragraphs describing his early life in Scotland and his university career, especially the important account of his first learning German and his early reading in German literature, where he found a new world in Goethe and Schiller.

Althaus was the first biographer to attempt to deal comprehensively with the influence of German thought on Carlyle. If modern scholarship has added a wealth of detail to the subject, his contribution remains that of the thoughtful pioneer who had fresh information. Supported by Carlyle's clarifying and supplementary comments, his discussion of

Carlyle's early investigation of German literature, though somewhat confused, has authority on this subject as no other has.[12] Narrative and notes complement—and in places seem to contradict—other accounts of Carlyle's first interest in German. The chief of these is a report of a conversation, of unknown date but probably after November 1876, with Arthur Penrhyn Stanley, Dean of Westminster, in which Carlyle recalls how he came to learn German:

> The first book that made me desire to know German was Madame de Stael's "Allemagne" [which he read in Sept. 1817]. She did not make it clear what it was that she thought so important in Germany, but she made me feel that there had been something which would solve all the questions with which I was tormented. It was very difficult to get any means of learning it. There was a Polish Jew who had taught that very distinguished man Edward Irving, but I could not get it from him. At last there was an old fellow-student of mine who agreed that we should make an exchange. He would teach me German and I would teach him French; and in that way I learned the pronunciation.[13]

On the surface, this statement contradicts an earlier one made in a letter to Goethe of 3 November 1829: "I still remember that it was the desire to read *Werner's* Mineralogical Doctrines in the original, that first set me on studying German; where truly I found a mine, far different from any of the Freyberg ones!"[14] Actually Carlyle's statements do not contradict each other: it *is* likely that Madame de Staël's work first made him wish to learn German, but the immediate stimulus was provided by his desire to read Werner in the original. During 1818–1819, Carlyle attended at the University the lectures on mineralogy given by Professor Robert Jameson, Werner's English disciple and the first exponent of his views in Britain,

12. Another recent account of Carlyle's first acquaintance with German is Rodger L. Tarr and Ian M. Campbell, "Carlyle's Early Study of German, 1819–1821," *Illinois Quarterly*, 34 (Dec. 1971), 19–27. It does not make use either of Althaus's biography or of Carlyle's notes.

13. Arthur A. Adrian, "Dean Stanley's Report of Conversations with Carlyle," *Victorian Studies*, 1 (Sept. 1957), 73–74.

14. Norton, *GC*, pp. 156–157. Werner is Abraham Gottlob Werner (1750–1817), the great German geologist; Freiberg in Saxony, famous for its nearby mines, maintained an Academy of Mines in which Werner taught. Emerson observes in *English Traits* that Carlyle turned to German on the advice of someone who told him that he would find what he wanted in that language.

and he wanted very much to penetrate beyond them to Werner himself. Whether Carlyle ever read Werner's works in the original is unknown, although it is known that his interest in mineralogy as a career ended with Jameson's lectures in the spring of 1819.

Althaus knew no other members of the Carlyle circle besides Neuberg, but he did examine conscientiously much of what he found already in print about Carlyle, chiefly John Sterling's early study in the *London and Westminster Review* (1839) and Thomas Ballantyne's "biographical memoir" prefacing his *Passages Selected from the Writings of Thomas Carlyle* (1855). He may have seen the biographical sketch of Carlyle, published anonymously but by R. H. Shepherd, in *On the Choice of Books* (1866), and other accounts as well. None would have afforded him much help. Neither the Sterling nor the Ballantyne gives many concrete facts about Carlyle's life (the few given are often inaccurate), and neither satisfies as biography. From Sterling's long article, which he cites several times, Althaus received a sound general estimate of Carlyle's achievement thus far and an evaluation of his importance for contemporaries. From Ballantyne's account he was led to Carlyle's 1828 letter to Goethe describing his life at Craigenputtoch and to Leigh Hunt's *Examiner* accounts of the 1838 and 1839 lectures. Both Sterling and Ballantyne knew Carlyle personally, Sterling very well, yet from the scantiness of the biographical information which they impart it is hardly surprising that Althaus felt compelled to seek out Neuberg in order to present a fuller, more accurate account.

By showing the interrelations among Carlyle's works, Althaus skillfully discerns the main lines of his career. He crams a considerable amount of information into the forty-one pages his narrative occupies in *Unsere Zeit*, yet throughout he preserves a just sense of balance in allotting space to biography and to works. He does not simply make use of facts on hand but tries to shape his material artistically. The chief weaknesses of his biography are those of the other early sketches of Carlyle: overreliance on *Sartor Resartus* as literal autobiography for the interpretation of the early years, and overindulgence in long quotations from the works to carry the argument. The quotations may perhaps be excused on the grounds that Althaus's German audience would not have been familiar with many of Carlyle's books. In any event, his selection of passages for quotation is excellent. More serious a charge is the unevenness of his criticism: passages of remarkable insight alternate with passages of awkward paraphrase. Although Althaus wrote his biography shortly after Carlyle's Edinburgh address and fifteen years before his death, he makes a careful attempt to set Carlyle's career within a historical perspective. By 1866, with the publication of *Frederick*, Carlyle had completed all his major works, and Althaus was thus able (though he could not have known it) to chronicle almost all that was of first importance in Carlyle's career. He has cogent points to make about many of the major essays and all of the major books.

Especially sure is his sense of Carlyle's development as a historian. He frequently cites his railings against the pedantry of contemporary historians, German as well as English, whom Carlyle designates as "dryasdusts." From the *French Revolution* to *Frederick*, he had challenged the older, fact-collecting schools of history by bodying forth in his own works the living essence of human beings once dynamically alive. Althaus, in interpreting Carlyle's histories, responded to their sense of intense energy kept under equally intense discipline. Although his evaluations are out of step with the modern consensus, which sees the *French Revolution* as Carlyle's masterpiece, they made sense in their day. Althaus praises *Cromwell* as the greatest of the histories and devotes considerable space to *Frederick*. In regard to *Cromwell*, he could not but be affected by the tremendous impact which Carlyle's history had had in overturning English prejudice against the Lord Protector and the Puritan side in the Civil Wars; in regard to *Frederick*, he knew a German audience would have a particular interest in Carlyle's most recent history and he was also writing at a time when many were hailing it as the triumph of his career.

Carlyle's notes to Althaus have value out of all proportion to their length. When he writes "Ach Gott!" in the margin opposite Althaus's account of the "deeds of heroism" perpetrated by the North in the American Civil War, those two words say more than would a paragraph. Like the other reminiscences, the notes to Althaus tell as much about Carlyle as about their ostensible subjects. And so Carlyle intended, for the Althaus as well as the Skirving reminiscence form part of a larger scheme, unplanned and never put into final shape by Carlyle, which constituted his major work after *Frederick*: the writing of the history of his life as it intertwined with that of his wife and with those of his family and friends. In the Althaus reminiscence, the interest often lies as much in what he does *not* say as in what he does. If he keeps returning to *Sartor*, we wonder why he is silent over the *Latter-Day Pamphlets*. Again, as we see in the other reminiscences, the events of his life before his removal to London in 1834 drew from him far more commentary than did those after. Probably he thought others would find his early years more interesting—certainly they interested him more—and the later years, in his eyes, had never fulfilled the hopes of the earlier. In his bereavement over his wife, he turned in memory again and again to the time of his young manhood when poor, solitary, nearly desperate, he struggled for existence and recognition in Edinburgh.

Carlyle wrote his notes in an abbreviated and elliptical style similar to that of the annotations to Mrs. Carlyle's letters published in Froude's edition of her *Letters and Memorials* and in Alexander Carlyle's edition of her *New Letters*. They are in the crabbed, minuscule hand of his old age familiar to students of his handwriting (see plates 2 and 3). He wrote carefully, on occasion with brilliance. With a deft phrase, a metaphor, an allusion, he conjures up before our eyes a picture of an event, a friend, a state of mind. Carlyle apparently read Althaus twice carefully, the first time making brief notes in pencil, the second time making detailed comments in ink and revising as he wrote. He may have looked the manuscript over a final time before putting it away. Restricted by the number and position of the interleaved sheets, he wrote tersely, saying the essential, no more. Thus his observations in Althaus are usually more condensed, occasionally more cryptic, than those in the other reminiscences. Stretching back more than sixty years, they evidence Carlyle's extraordinary memory in recalling the minutest details of his intellectual history and personal life. His veneration of fact impels him to strive for accuracy, and if in his notes his memory on occasion fails him for a date, his recollection of the sequence of events is usually without fault.

Ranging from the correction of a phrase to page-long evocations of events, the notes provide an unusual glimpse into Carlyle's mind and art. In them, he speaks candidly of his friends, books, literary opinions, and of much else. That he fully intended them to be used by subsequent biographers his preface makes clear. "The *fewer* errors they set afloat . . . on this subject, the better it will be," he writes there, and concludes in the afterword: "Here and there a bit of certainty may have its advantages." Some of the notes served as trial runs for incidents more fully narrated in the other reminiscences, in particular "Edward Irving," which he began soon after he completed the Althaus. Indeed, it is likely that putting down his commentary to Althaus's biography gave Carlyle the idea to write the Irving reminiscence. Stimulated by the biography to look inward, he wrote the notes as a first thinking-through of much that he found painful to recall. Although the comments on *Sartor* deserve pride of place, they are challenged by the pen portraits of Irving, his own father and mother, and, most moving of all, his superb evocation of his brother Alexander. In swift strokes, he summons up the homely joys and obscure destiny of the brother who lived to fame unknown, staying behind on the farm while he went off to study in Edinburgh. Always a shadowy figure, Alick, next in age to Carlyle, comes to life here as nowhere else.

It is to *Sartor* that Carlyle directs his most illuminating remarks. Since he has little to say about it in the other reminiscences, unquestionably he meant his comments in Althaus to constitute his major statement. Despite his later professed depreciation of *Sartor*, he may have unconsciously divined that it was to be his most enduring work. While he explains in several letters what he is attempting to do in *Sartor*, only in the interleaved Althaus does he discuss its autobiographical significance.[15]

Perhaps alone of Carlyle's biographers, Froude was able to view *Sartor* within the perspective of his entire career. With his excellent command of German, he could read Althaus's biography as he studied Carlyle's notes. Many of them, even when not directly quoted in his first volume, are subsumed within his narrative or inform his discussion. Passages from these notes in Froude's biography that are familiar to students of Carlyle— most of all, the passages in which Carlyle speaks of *Sartor*—will take on new and occasionally unexpected meaning when read in the way Froude read them. The passages on *Sartor* convinced him that Carlyle had based many incidents in the book on real-life experiences.

Alexander Carlyle, Carlyle's nephew, concurred. In a long appendix to his two-volume edition of the *Love Letters of Thomas Carlyle and Jane Welsh*, he affirmed *Sartor*'s value "as an autobiography of Carlyle in his early years" (II, 361) and on several occasions quoted in support of his views Carlyle's notes to Althaus. Critics since then have often ignored or denied the autobiographical elements of *Sartor*. Yet it is not necessary that *Sartor* be interpreted as literal autobiography to realize that Alexander Carlyle hardly exaggerates when he contends that chapters 5 through 9 of Book II are "founded on incidents and experiences in Carlyle's own history" and are "in fact a sort of autobiography for the period mentioned,

15. See my article "Carlyle on *Sartor Resartus*," forthcoming in *New Essays on Carlyle*, ed. Kenneth J. Fielding and Rodger L. Tarr.

delineated poetically, spiritually and figuratively, yet true to life as regards the chief incidents and events, and not far from the truth even in the details" (II, 366). Indeed, his contention derives its chief support from Carlyle's own carefully considered observations. Their publication here, set within the context of the Althaus biography, should help to clarify the extent to which *Sartor* is autobiography.

No other biographer or critic of Carlyle besides Froude and Alexander Carlyle has, to my knowledge, made use of the comments in the interleaved Althaus. Why both Froude and Charles Eliot Norton omitted the notes to Althaus in the editions they prepared of Carlyle's other reminiscences must remain a matter for conjecture. Presenting them clearly would have been the major problem. It may have been impractical to translate the Althaus biography, and without the biography the notes read like half of a dialogue. Norton was certainly aware of their existence, but he limited himself to citing a few passages in the volumes of Carlyle's correspondence and reminiscences which he edited. He appears to be the last person outside the Carlyle family to have seen them. Even David Alec Wilson, a close friend of the younger Alexander Carlyle, did not have access to the interleaved Althaus in preparing his monumental six-volume biography of Carlyle (1923–1934).[16] Not only, then, do the notes to Althaus constitute a major document for understanding Carlyle's life, but they also provide one of the few instances in literary biography in which the subject of the biography had the opportunity to comment extensively on his biographer's account. And when that person is Carlyle, whose writings on the art of biography have been influential and controversial and who doubted that anyone would ever know his own "poor 'Biography,'" the comments should prove significant within the history of literary biography.

It is ironic in the context of Carlyle's explosion in "Sir Walter Scott" (1838) on the mealy-mouthed respectability of English biography that Froude, his chosen biographer, published after his death a life so frank in its revelations that it caused a major Victorian scandal which reverberated strongly for fifty years and whose echoes still have not altogether died away. Carlyle saw biography as the truest as well as one of the noblest of the literary arts, valuing it, for instance, far more highly than poetry. Biography he considered the essence of history and he insisted that it reveal

16. He refers to its existence in vol. VI, 124, 194.

history, that it be true to the spirit of the times as well as to the facts of a man's existence. Good biography, therefore, must reproduce not only the life of the individual but also the life of the society flowing around him.

The paradox in Carlyle's attitude toward his own biography is the indifference or hostility he expressed toward the prospect of anyone writing it. Yet he must have secretly wished that someone would write it, or at least interpret it in a way he could in part determine beforehand. That he included a preface and afterword to the Althaus biography indicates that he judged it in some degree valid as an interpretation of his life. It remains the closest we have—with the conjectural exception of Froude—to an authorized or approved biography. Although Carlyle felt that Althaus had done a creditable job, there remained a great deal he did not know and could hardly be expected to know. Perhaps it was while writing the commentary to Althaus that Carlyle realized it had to be supplemented still more. It is even possible, though unlikely, that he might not have written his other autobiographical writings if the Althaus biography had not crossed his path when it did. In any event, Carlyle came to realize the necessity of clarifying many points in his life that would be obscure to the inevitable biographers of the future. No other explanation begins to account for his protracted labors in the years following his wife's death when he wrote the reminiscences and edited her correspondence. Only through this work could he put his own life into perspective and attempt to come to terms with it. That his biography be accurate explains his careful correction of dates and statements in Althaus's account; that it be true explains his clarifying and interpretive comments. Yet on the ultimate dimension—that a biographer could represent the essence of his life—on that he despaired. Perhaps the underlying motive behind his decision to entrust his literary remains to Froude, to use as he saw fit, was that he believed Froude to be, after all, the person best able to understand him and his achievement within the history of his own times. Although Althaus possessed nowhere near Froude's literary skill or his sense of the drama of human events, his work, which proved of considerable service to Froude, is a worthy forerunner to its huge successor.

Note on the Text

In the 1870's, along with Carlyle's other personal papers, the interleaved copy of Althaus's biography came into the hands of Froude. Upon completion in 1884 of his four-volume life, he returned Carlyle's papers to Mary Aitken Carlyle, Carlyle's niece. When she died in 1895, it remained in the possession of her husband, Alexander Carlyle, until his death in 1931. On 14 June 1932 the manuscript was sold as part of lot 203 at the great Sotheby sale of Carlyle's books, letters, and manuscripts. It brought £23, a fraction of what it would bring today. Lot 203 also included a typed translation of Althaus's biography, two typed copies of Carlyle's notes, two letters from Althaus to Carlyle, and other biographical material by Carlyle or relating to him. In April 1934 the National Library of Scotland purchased the interleaved Althaus from Messrs. Maggs, along with a typed copy by Alexander Carlyle of most of Carlyle's notes. The Library did not purchase the other items in lot 203, and I am unaware of their present whereabouts. The interleaved Althaus and Alexander Carlyle's typed copy are now catalogued as MS 1799 and MS 1800. The text of this edition I base on MS 1799.

Editorial policies followed in this volume are designed to present a text that is both readable and reasonably faithful to the original. Althaus's biography is written in a nineteenth-century academic prose, careful, pondered, the sentences involuted, often very long—so long that many I have had to break up into two, three, sometimes four English sentences. As Althaus republished his biography in *Englische Charakterbilder* (1869), I have collated the text there against that in *Unsere Zeit* (1866) and have indicated in my notes wherever in the later version he modifies a statement in the earlier. Carlyle corrected a few printer's errors in the *Unsere Zeit* version; others he let stand. Those that involve a change in the meaning of a word I have footnoted; those that concern lesser matters such as spelling I have silently incorporated into the translation. I saw no need to repeat the outdated bibliographical citations in several of Althaus's footnotes and have given in their place references to standard texts. Only the more misleading of his statements about Carlyle's life and works are corrected in the notes; to have dealt with them all would have entailed a considerable increase in the number of notes. Althaus is inconsistent about quotation marks: sometimes he uses them when he paraphrases Carlyle, at other times he does not use them when he quotes him. In the first instance I have removed the quotation marks and in the second added them. Whenever I have identified a passage as Carlyle's—or whenever Althaus attempts a close paraphrase—I have given Carlyle's own words.

Carlyle's notes receive full editorial consideration, especially when they contradict generally held views of him or provide a new interpretation of an event, person or work. I have tried to fill in background succinctly, to answer obvious questions, and to indicate related passages in Carlyle's *Reminiscences* and in his other writings. I have also thought it best to indicate wherever a passage has been published or alluded to in Froude's biography. References to modern scholarship have been kept to a minimum. Carlyle's notes are published as he wrote them, except that his abbreviations have usually been expanded. I saw no valid reason to make them an unnecessary hurdle to readers unfamiliar with them. Thus in the manuscript "Edinburgh" is written "Edin^r," "merchant" "merch^t," "which" "wh^h," etc. Words crossed out, when legible and when significant, have been placed in brackets following the substituted word and so designated. Carlyle's punctuation has not been altered; I usually provide, however, terminal punctuation for his notes in instances when he has not. His usage of single and double quotation marks has been observed and his spellings followed (except that "Kirkaldy" is always spelled "Kirkcaldy" and "Craigenputtock" "Craigenputtoch"). Overworking "*sic*" has been avoided. While Carlyle occasionally marked several places in Althaus's text as applicable for a single note, I have placed an asterisk only at the first indication. Rarely did I have to guess where a note had to be attached. On those few occasions when they did not concern matters of content I have omitted Carlyle's directions concerning his note, e.g., "see leaf at right." In a few places where the manuscript has almost disintegrated I have had to follow Alexander Carlyle's transcription.

[*Carlyle's Preface*]

The following German Sketch of me was received here, and read with little interest, tho' with recognition of the Author's kind intentions, some two months ago. I had heard of Althaus & his project, a good while before, thro' Neuberg; who put many questions on his behalf,—to little purpose, as would seem. Three weeks ago, on making ready for "Ripple-Court, & my fortnight of idle sea-bathing," I bethought me of having the poor Piece *interleaved* in this manner, and of perhaps correcting one or two blunders here & there. At Ripple Court my idleness was complete; but it was also *strenuous* per force,[1] every moment of it "*occupied with doing nothing*"; very sickly too;—so, on the whole, there was little or no sea-bathing to be got at; and of correcting Althaus absolutely none at all. At home today, in the solitudes & silences, two days after my return, I take up Althaus again; and will glance him over, pen in hand, should anything easily correctible turn up. Of incorrectible, or not easily correctible there will be very much; but this, on the whole, is considerably the best Sketch I have yet seen on the subject;—and every error that one slays on any subject is a good turn, or the potentiality of one. Nobody, as I have often said, will ever know my poor "Biography": but probably various persons will make attempts upon it, after I am gone; and certainly the *fewer* errors they set afloat, among the idle or the studious & considerate, on this subject, the better it will be so far.— — Althaus, I hear, is a man towards 40; some kind of German Teacher in Woolwich Military Academy, and 'own Correspondent' of various German Newspapers; a perfectly respectable and quietly diligent Householder & Pater-familias among us. —T.C. (Chelsea, 29 August 1866).

1. Horace, *Epistles*, I, xi, 28: "strenua inertia."

In comparing the genius of the English people (as it reveals itself in history or culminates[2] in particularly outstanding individuals) with the genius of other peoples, we can say in general that the former is remarkable more for its outstanding concentration than for its humanistic breadth, more for its energetic realism than for the ultimate depth of its character and its actions. This contrast is sharpest in scholarship, philosophy, and the writing of history. Other nations—the German, the French, the Italian—boast of their genius for the universal and quite naturally take pleasure in the development of vast systems of thought, cosmic constructions of the first origins and ultimate purposes of the world and man, which from time to time have issued forth from the workshops of their great thinkers. With the English, on the other hand, all such attempts to present the world and man in a comprehensive relationship to one another and to build all existing reality from the mind create at the outset a vague feeling of skepticism and distrust, a feeling rooted in the deep-seated conviction that human powers are inadequate for so great an undertaking. In fact, both the philosophy and the ordinary way of thinking of the English people are essentially inductive. Her intellectual leaders can by and large be designated as first-rate specialists. Rather than venture into universal history or even into the philosophy of history, her historians prefer to specialize in narrow fields of professional interest. Her educators, in the last analysis, work from similar premises. Historically, the result of this way of thinking has been a human understanding that is self-assured, bold, persevering, practical and healthy, but which, while gladly foregoing adventuresome flights of thought and refraining from plumbing ultimate depths of feeling, still claims all the stronger an influence and all the more powerful a mastery in the real world.

Yet if we admit the correctness of this view by and large, it has, like

2. "Cultivirt" (cultivates) changed by Carlyle to "culminirt"; similarly changed in Althaus (1869).

every general description, its significant exceptions and qualifications. Even the idealistically-inclined Germans have produced their practical heroes, and even mighty England has its transcendental philosophers. To this tendency has been joined the astonishing development of international trade in our day. It has furthered at the same time the exchange of the products of commerce and industry and the dissemination of humanistic ideas and culture. Its growth had already matured during the twenty years in which the patriarch Goethe brought to maturity his thoughts on the origin of a "world literature."[3] The influence of this course of development upon the ways of thinking of individual nations must to be sure remain inherently slow. But its efficacy in wide circles is such an undisputed fact that it would be impossible to appreciate fully the significance and character of the extraordinary man who forms the subject of this sketch without taking into account the cultural influence which those international relations of "world literature" exerted upon him. With his national inheritance having little evident influence upon him, all strands of the spiritual being of Thomas Carlyle, the English journalist,*

* schwerlich [*hardly*]![4]

humorist, philosopher and historian, find roots deep in the soil of our German philosophy and literature. Despite the contrast to that particular English genius which we mentioned earlier, he has gained for himself a place among the leading literary figures and, what is more, has influenced the development of thought in his native land—an achievement that is as far-reaching and remarkable as it is, in its own way, unrivaled. Goethe first set forth in detail his ideas on "world literature" in the preface to the German translation of Carlyle's *Life of Schiller*,[5] and the cross-fertilization which has since taken place between German and English literature and culture is too well-known to require at this point more than

3. A concept to which Carlyle responded enthusiastically in his essays on German subjects of the late 1820's and early 1830's. Goethe's various pronouncements on "world literature" are recorded in an appendix to Fritz Strich, *Goethe and World Literature* (1949), trans. C. A. M. Sym.

4. "Schwerlich!" may possibly apply to Carlyle's seeing himself called "English" as well as "journalist."

5. Published in 1830. Goethe had expressed to Carlyle the concept of world literature in his letter of 20 July 1827 (unpublished at the time Althaus wrote his biography). See *CL*, IV, 211.

passing reference. Without question the Germans have done better in this international endeavor to assimilate foreign culture. But even among our people who are so well endowed with this power of cultural synthesis, it is doubtful whether English literature has ever had as profound an effect upon the genius of an outstanding man as German literature has had upon Carlyle's genius. Under no circumstances would we contend that the impact of this combination exhaustively characterizes Carlyle's significance for literary history. By nature, he had far too individual a spirit, far too resolute, uninhibited and independent a talent, ever to surrender his originality in a sentimental devotion to the study of a foreign literature. Yet his affinity to German literature and philosophy is a basic trait of the man himself and comes inevitably to the fore in any consideration of his literary activity. And while English criticism has used this as the pretext for much justified censure, German criticism has derived from it a bond of an almost personal nature to Carlyle that facilitates an understanding of his achievements and individuality.

Thomas Carlyle was born on the fourth of December 1795 in Ecclefechan, a village in Dumfriesshire in the south of Scotland. His father was a prosperous farmer and a man of remarkable* gifts of mind

* Considerably the *most "bedeutend"* I have ever met with in my journey thro' life. Sterling *veracity*, in thought, in word, and in deed; *courage* mostly quiet, but capable of blazing into fire-whirlwinds when needful: these, and such a flash of just *insight*, and of brief natural eloquence and emphasis, true to every feature, as I have never met with in any other man (myself included) were the leading features of him.[6] 'Humour,' of a most grim Scandinavian type, he occasionally had; 'wit' rarely or never, too serious for 'wit.' My excellent Mother, with perhaps the deeper *piety* in most senses, had also the most *sport*,—of what is called wit, humour &c. No man of my day, or hardly any man, can have had better parents.

6. Cf. *Reminiscences*, II, 305: "My Father's [delineations of people], in rugged simple force, picturesque ingenuity, veracity and brevity, were, I do judge, superior to even Wordsworth's, as bits of human Portraiture." Carlyle's characterization of his father in Althaus (paraphrased and quoted in Froude, *Carlyle*, I, 11) should be compared to the fuller portrait, written immediately after his father's death in 1832, in *Reminiscences*, I, 1–52. Cf. also *Reminiscences*, I, 153–154.

and character, who among his neighbors came to be taken as a kind of oracle.* He was distinguished for the seriousness of his religious con-

*Didn't much; nor ever wished to do it: had a great contempt (*verachtung ja nicht-achtung* [*scorn, even want of regard*]) for "Public Opinion";—a trait that has *not* been quite lost perhaps!

victions and for his practical understanding and rich vein of biting humor and wit. His mother was well-known for her intelligence, her piety, and a gentle affectionate heart—qualities which accorded perfectly with those of his father. Taken together, they include nearly all the spiritual traits from which the character of the son developed. In addition to this family background, we must keep in mind the nature of the land and the people in whose midst the child grew up. Even now, in spite of all the advances of modern civilization, Scotland has preserved much of the rough, rugged, dark and magnificent character of its Ossianic prehistory; even now, as in the sixteenth and seventeenth centuries, it remains ·the classic land of Puritanism, where the solemn and strict ways of the times of John Knox and Oliver Cromwell endure more nearly unchanged than anywhere else in England. These circumstances provide a key to many characteristic features of Thomas Carlyle as author and as human being. Indeed, his entire development and way of thinking reflect clearly the influence of those traits of his Scots nationality. His imagination, put to the test on the widest possible variety of subjects, bears a distinctly Ossianic coloring; his personality, though it rests on essentially contemporary assumptions of philosophy and culture, calls to mind unmistakably the ancient Puritan figures of the period of the Reformation and the Civil Wars in the history of England and Scotland. The only intellectual leaders of his tiny native land who in this respect are at all comparable to him are Robert Burns and Sir Walter Scott. But neither Burns nor Scott commands the humor and the poetic imagination which emerge with such trenchant, energetic and outstanding originality of thought in Thomas Carlyle.

Little is known of Carlyle's youth. If we can (probably not incorrectly) apply essentially to himself the biographical sketch he gives of Professor Teufelsdröckh in *Sartor Resartus*, he gave hint early of a contemplative melancholy nature.* "Thus encircled by the mystery of Existence,"

Sartor is quite unsafe for details! Fiction *founded* perhaps on fact—a long way off.[7]

7. Cf. Froude, *Carlyle*, I, 15 and 26.

he has his hero say in *Sartor*,

> under the deep heavenly Firmament; waited-on by the four golden Seasons, with their vicissitudes of contribution, for even grim Winter brought its skating-matches and shooting-matches, its snow-storms and Christmas-carols,—did the Child sit and learn. These things were the Alphabet, whereby in aftertime he was to syllable and partly read the grand Volume of the World: what matters it whether such Alphabet be in large gilt letters or in small ungilt ones, so you have an eye to read it? For Gneschen, eager to learn, the very act of looking thereon was a blessedness that gilded all: his existence was a bright, soft element of Joy; out of which, as in Prospero's Island, wonder after wonder bodied itself forth, to teach by charming.

> Nevertheless, I were but a vain dreamer to say, that even then my felicity was perfect. I had, once for all, come down from Heaven into the Earth. Among the rainbow colours that glowed on my horizon, lay even in childhood a dark ring of Care, as yet no thicker than a thread, and often quite overshone; yet always it reappeared, nay ever waxing broader and broader; till in after-years it almost over-shadowed my whole canopy, and threatened to engulf me in final night. It was the ring of Necessity whereby we are all begirt; happy he for whom a kind heavenly Sun brightens it into a ring of Duty, and plays round it with beautiful prismatic diffractions; yet ever, as basis and as bourne for our whole being, it is there.[8]

Endowed (as these words show) with a deep feeling for the beauty and the mystery of the world around him, the boy grew up, earnest and pensive, in his home town in Dumfriesshire in the south of Scotland. Life in the parental home was austere, rigorous and frugal, but with all its limitations loving and harmonious and, on the whole, eminently suited to establish in his soul a firm base for the future. In fact, he often acknowledged on later occasions his inestimable good fortune in having had such an upbringing and how much he owed to the teaching and example of his father and mother.

Carlyle received his first instruction in the village school of Ecclefechan.* At the same time he also studied Latin with the village

* This is hardly correct. My Mother had taught me reading, I never remembered when. "Tom Donaldson's School" at

8. Harrold, *Sartor*, pp. 97–98.

Ecclefechan,—a severely correct young man, Tom; from Edinburgh College, one session probably; went afterwards to Manchester &c, & I never saw his face again, tho' I still remember it well, as always merry & kind to me, tho' harsh & to the ill-deserving[9] severe. Hoddam School afterwards; which then stood at the Kirk. "Sandy Beattie" (subsequently a Burgher Minister in Glasgow; I well remember his "examining" us that day) reported me "complete in English," age then about 7; that I must "go into Latin," or waste my time: Latin accordingly; with what enthusiasm! But the poor Schoolmaster did not himself know Latin; I gradually got altogether swamped and bewildered under him; reverend Mr Johnstone of Ecclefechan (or *first*, his son, home from College, and already teaching a young Nephew or Cousin, in a careless but intelligent manner) had to take me in hand; and, once pulled afloat again, I made rapid & sure way: a most exact & faithful man Mr Johnstone Senior; my Father & Mother's Minister (Burgher), both of whom he esteemed. The venerablest & most venerated Clerical Person I have ever seen. White full bottom Wig; income £75 to £100 a year.[10]

minister, a circumstance which suggests that a scholarly career was already under consideration for him. He learned easily and combined at an early age his brooding contemplative nature with a restless intellectual curiosity, which manifested itself as much in his lively interest in all the incidents of daily life as in a bent for reading of various kinds. The minister therefore thought that he must make a scholar out of him, a divinity student if possible, and to carry out these plans Carlyle was sent in his eleventh year (1806)* to the Grammar School in the neighboring

* 26 May 1806, a bright sunny morning: which I still vividly remember.[11]

town of Annan. How he fared there *Sartor Resartus* hints at in an easily recognizable way. "I was among strangers," he has Professor Teufelsdröckh

9. "Undeserving" in Froude, *Carlyle*, I, 17.

10. Passage published in Froude, *Carlyle*, I, 16–17, and in part in *LL*, II, 369. References in the *CL* to the Rev. Mr. Johnstone are few, but see *Reminiscences*, I, 40–41; II, 13–14; and "Unpublished Letters of Carlyle," *Scribner's Magazine*, 13 (April 1893), 422.

11. Quoted in Froude, *Carlyle*, I, 17. See *Reminiscences*, I, 46, and cf. Harrold, *Sartor*, p. 103.

say of himself.[12] He disliked the wild, rough ways of his schoolmates. He did not take part in their games and "wept often; indeed to such a degree that he was nicknamed *Der Weinende* (the Tearful), which epithet, till towards his thirteenth year, was indeed not quite unmerited."[13] "My Teachers," he says in another passage, "were hide-bound Pedants, without knowledge of man's nature, or of boy's. . . . Innumerable dead Vocables . . . they crammed into us, and called it fostering the growth of mind. . . . Greek and Latin were 'mechanically' taught; Hebrew scarce even mechanically; much else which they called History, Cosmography, Philosophy, and so forth, no better than not at all.[14] So that, except inasmuch as . . . he himself 'went about, as was of old his wont, among the Craftsmen's workshops, there learning many things,'"[15] and diligently read a great deal on his own, "his time, it would appear, was utterly wasted."[16] Who does not already recognize in these traits the prototype of the sensitive soul, the stern, dissatisfied, idealistic, resigned "weeping philosopher" of later years?[17] Even if his discontented spirit sought refuge from the routine of school existence in tasks that he picked out for himself and in the workshops of the real world, still the solid learning acquired in his school years did not serve him badly.* His memory was as

* *Sartor* here, in good part;[18] not to be trusted in details! "Greek," for example, consisted of the *Alphabet* mainly; "Hebrew" is quite a *German* entity,—nobody in that region, except my reverend old Mr Johnstone, could have read one sentence of it to save his life. I did get to read Latin & French with fluency (Latin *quantity* was left a frightful chaos, and I had to learn it afterwards); some geometry, algebra (*arithmetic* thoroughly well), vague outlines of geography &c I did learn;—all the Books I could get were also

12. Harrold, *Sartor*, p. 103.
13. Ibid., p. 104. Harrold notes that the passage is autobiographical.
14. Ibid., pp. 105, 104.
15. Ibid., p. 104. Harrold notes Goethe's similar experience, cited by Carlyle in *Works*, XXVII, 415.
16. Ibid., p. 104.
17. Heraclitus (c. 540–c. 470 B.C.), known as the "Weeping Philosopher."
18. "Here, in good part" omitted in Froude, *Carlyle*, I, 17. C. E. Norton and A. Carlyle publish part of this passage accurately (*Reminiscences*, II, 16, and *LL*, II, 365). Writers on Carlyle who have quoted Froude's text miss the fundamental change in emphasis caused by the omitted words. "Here" refers to Carlyle's experiences in Annan Academy, 1806–1809.

devoured; but my "Hang" [*the "bent toward abstract reflection" mentioned below by Althaus*] there is a myth.[19] Mythically *true* is what Sartor says of his Schoolfellows, and not half of the truth. Unspeakable is the damage & defilement I got out of those coarse unguided tyrannous cubs,—especially till I revolted against them, and gave stroke for stroke; as my pious Mother, in her great love of peace and of my best interests, spiritual chiefly, had imprudently forbidden me to do. One way and another I had never been so wretched as here in that School, and the first 2 years of my time in it still count among the miserable of my life. "Academies," "High Schools," "Instructors of Youth"—Oh ye unspeakable!—

retentive as his diligence and ability to learn were great. Moreover, since he had in equal measure the gift of being able to cope with a mass of details and the bent toward abstract reflection, he also mastered the dry subjects in the school curriculum and after just three years was graduated from Annan Grammar School to go to the University of Edinburgh.

His parents, as noted, had destined him for the ministry. However, the faculties in English and Scottish universities are less strictly separated than in Germany, and even the traditional departments of Classics and Mathematics also serve, first of all, as the chief subjects for the study of divinity. We do not have more detailed knowledge of Carlyle's classical studies; one also looks in vain in his whole later development for a spiritual reflection of ancient life and literature.* From the beginning it

* Knew nothing of it, for years after leaving College;—little about it still tho' always rather learning. Homer *in original* (read with difficulty), after *Wolf*'s broad flash of light thrown into it;[20]

19. "But my 'Hang' there is a myth" omitted in Froude, *Carlyle*, I, 17. Carlyle in effect affirms that in his youth he was more firmly rooted in the everyday world than Althaus (and later biographers) realized.

20. Friedrich August Wolf (1759–1824), *Prolegomena ad Homerum* . . . (Halle, 1795), vol. I. Cf. *Works*, XXIX, 93. In January 1834, while still at Craigenputtoch, Carlyle began to read the *Iliad* in the original Greek under the supervision of William Glen and continued reading through the spring. On 18 April he wrote Leigh Hunt: "I am writing *nothing*; reading, above all things, my old *Homer* and Prolegomena enough; the old song itself with a most singular delight" (Charles Richard Sanders, *The Correspondence and Friendship of Thomas Carlyle and Leigh Hunt* [Manchester: The John Rylands Library, 1963], p. 28). Cf. Carlyle's journal entries in Froude, *Carlyle*, II, 404–406, and, for his opinions on Greek literature in general, the first two of the *Lectures on the History of Literature*, ed. J. Reay Greene (New York: Scribner's, 1892).

Aeschylus, Sophocles (mainly in translations); *item* [*likewise*]
partly Tacitus, Virgil, &c &c, became really interesting to me;
Homer & Aeschylus, above all. Horace, '*egoistisch, leichtlebig*'
[*egoistical, easy-going*] in sad fact, I never cared for. Cicero, after
long & various trials, has always proved a windy person and a
wearisome to me: extinguished altogether, quite recently, by
Middleton's excellent tho' misjudging *Life* of him.[21] In the Classics
field I am truly as Nothing. At this day, Clough's *Plutarch*.[22]

appears that this world lay far from his interests, or else did not arouse
his sympathies. Perhaps its naively egotistical, easy-going character was
distasteful to him even in his youth. Certainly, later historical periods—
the Middle Ages, the Reformation, the French Revolution—were to
have a continuing and deeper influence on a temperament that in its
innermost core sensed with shattering force the disparity between Nature
and Spirit. It struggled with passionate energy for a reconciliation of
the conflicting elements and for a practical guiding principle in the
disordered chaos of the world in which destiny had placed him. On
the other hand, he studied mathematics with great enthusiasm and just
as eagerly* took part in the philosophical debates, which were then

* *Not* now at all; and '*eifrig*' never. 'Dugald Stewart' had gone,
the year before I entered:[23] my Professorial Lecturer was Thomas
Brown;[24] an eloquent acute little gentleman; full of enthusiasm
about 'simple suggestion' & 'relative' ditto,—to me unprofitable
utterly & bewildering & dispiriting 'as the autumn winds among
the withered leaves.'[25] "*Sonate, que me veux-tu?*" [*Sonate, what*

21. Conyers Middleton, *The History of the Life of Marcus Tullius Cicero*, 2 vols.
(London, 1741). Many subsequent editions.

22. *Plutarch's Lives. The translation called Dryden's* . . . revised by A. H. Clough
(London, 1864). Cf. Froude, *Carlyle*, I, 25.

23. Dugald Stewart (1753–1828). Carlyle began his university studies in the winter
term of 1809 and his study of moral philosophy in the winter term of 1810. Stewart
retired as professor of moral philosophy at the end of the spring term of 1809.

24. Thomas Brown (1778–1820) was appointed Stewart's coadjutor in 1809 but
undertook the full duties of the position. In 1810 he was elected Stewart's colleague;
Stewart supported Brown's candidacy but later became dissatisfied with his teaching.

25. Cf. Froude, *Carlyle*, I, 25. Perhaps a distant echo of Dante, *Inferno*, III, 109–112,
or of *Paradise Lost*, I, 302–306: "Thick as autumnal leaves that strow the brooks / In
Vallombrosa . . . or scattered sedge / Afloat, when with fierce winds. . . ."

do you wish with me?]26— — Except Leslie in Mathematics no Professor did me almost any good.

presided over in Edinburgh by Dugald Stewart and which had earned for the "Athens of the North" a reputation for rationalism and freedom of thought. However, to judge by comments made by Professor Teufelsdröckh in *Sartor Resartus*, even these studies—and the whole university experience as well—left his soul unsatisfied and still thirsting for the highest. "'The hungry young,'" he says,

'looked up to their spiritual Nurses; and, for food, were bidden eat the eastwind. What vain jargon of controversial Metaphysic, Etymology, and mechanical Manipulation falsely named Science, was current there, I indeed learned, better perhaps than the most. Among eleven-hundred Christian youths, there will not be wanting some eleven eager to learn. By collision with such, a certain warmth, a certain polish was communicated; by instinct and happy accident, I took less to rioting (*renommiren*), than to thinking and reading, which latter also I was free to do. Nay from the chaos of that Library, I succeeded in fishing-up more books perhaps than had been known to the very keepers thereof. The foundation of a Literary Life was hereby laid. I learned, on my own strength, to read fluently in almost all cultivated languages, on almost all subjects and sciences; farther, as man is ever the prime object to man, already it was my favourite employment to read character in speculation, and from the Writing to construe the Writer. A certain groundplan of Human Nature and Life began to fashion itself in me; wondrous enough, now when I look back on it; for my whole Universe, physical and spiritual, was as yet a Machine! However, such a conscious, recognized groundplan ... *was* beginning to be there, and by additional experiments might be corrected and indefinitely extended.'27

In the meantime, his satisfaction with these achievements did not last long. The universe, viewed as a machine through the medium of rationalism, left his passionate young heart discontented. But he was also incapable of returning to his childhood beliefs. "'Fever-paroxysms of Doubt'"28

26. A comment attributed to Bernard le Bouvier de Fontenelle (1657–1757), who was irritated by the music ("sonata" in the etymological sense of the word, i.e., playing a wind or stringed instrument).
27. Harrold, *Sartor*, p. 113.
28. Ibid., p. 114.

alternated successively with examinations of the miracles and the proofs of religious faith, and the striving to find serenity and peace ended in a restless skepticism.

Thus the university years went by, in strenuous studies of a general kind, in religious conflicts, and in extreme solitude. It remains unclear whether in the meantime the preliminary steps toward the furthering of his theological career* took place, or were definitely given up, or were

* In me it never was in any favour; tho' my Parents silently much wished it, as I knew well. Finding I had objections, my Father, with a magnanimity which I admired and admire, left me frankly to my own guidance in that matter, as did my Mother (probably still more lovingly, tho' not so silently); and the "theological course" (which *could* be prosecuted, or kept open, by appearing annually, putting down your name, with some trifling fee, in the Register, and then going your ways) was, after perhaps 2 years of this languid form, allowed to close itself for good. I remember yet being on the street in Argyll Square, Edinburgh (probably in 1817,[29] & come over from Kirkcaldy), with some intent, the languidest possible, still to put down my name & fee: the Official person, when I rang, was not at home;—and my instant feeling was, "Very good, then, *very* good; let this be *finis* in the matter,"— and it neatly was.[30]

only postponed for a while. This last possibility is the most likely. For a nature as profound and severe as Carlyle's, a skeptical attitude could not suffice in the long run. Nor could it be expected that the magnificent ruins of the old world, whose mysterious being still breathed upon him in the midst of decay, should be quickly swept away or quickly replaced by the creation of a universe based on the spirit. *Sartor Resartus*, the work in which he set down the history of his inner conflicts and which in a certain sense may serve as their reconciliation and as the most important turning-point in his development, was only written sixteen years after the end of his academic studies. Therefore, we have still to think of him for a long time during this interval in the image of the prophets who 'twixt

29. March 1817. The "Official person" was Dr. William Ritchie (1747–1830), professor of divinity at Edinburgh. Cf. *Reminiscences*, II, 39, and *CL*, I, 97.

30. Cf. Froude, *Carlyle*, I, 54. See also Ian M. Campbell, "Portrait of Carlyle," *The Scotsman*, 12 Aug. 1967, p. 3.

night and dawn wander amid ruins toward the day, although the choice of his life's work, the external manifestation of his destiny, had already been made many years before this time.

As the next biographical fact, it is clear that Carlyle, soon after the end*

* (for the present)

of his university years (1813 or** 1814), accepted a position as mathematics

** [*Carlyle crosses out "1813 or" and writes*] Summer.

teacher at Annan Grammar School. His parents' means were such that—after the necessarily expensive existence at the University—the son's early financial independence appeared desirable. As far as he was concerned, with his Faustian temperament, he found himself, though a teacher of the most exact of all disciplines, in the humiliating position of "having to say what he did not know." Yet, apart from these considerations, his early liking for mathematics is also a matter of interest.* It doesn't

* Perhaps it was mainly the accident that poor Leslie, alone of my Professors, had some genius in his business, and awoke a certain enthusiasm in me. For several years, from 1813 onwards (perhaps 7 in *all*), "Geometry" shone before me as undoubtedly the *noblest* of all sciences; and I prosecuted it (or Mathematics generally) in all my best hours and moods,—tho' far more pregnant inquiries were rising in me, and gradually *engrossing* me, *heart* as well as head. So that, about 1820 or '21, I had entirely thrown Mathematics aside; and, except in one or two brief spurts, lasting perhaps a couple of days, and more or less of a morbid nature, have never in the least regarded it farther.[31]

often happen that both the historical and the mathematical imagination inhabit the same mind, and if on the other hand the mathematician can walk arm in arm with the philosopher a good part of the way, he rarely will overleap the boundary which divides the realm of mathematical understanding from that of abstract thought. In Carlyle's development we see, however, these usually disparate talents united in a fruitful

31. Cf. Froude, *Carlyle*, I, 26, and Norton, *GC*, pp. 156–157. Professor John Leslie (1766–1832), Scottish mathematician and physicist, acknowledged in the 3rd ed. (1817) of his *Elements of Geometry* that the solution of an important problem had been "suggested to me by Mr. Thomas Carlyle, an ingenious young mathematician, formerly my pupil" (p. 340). See Peter A. Wursthorn, "The Position of Thomas Carlyle in the History of Mathematics," *The Mathematics Teacher*, 59 (Dec. 1966), 755–770.

reciprocity: the mathematician lends a hand to the philosopher, the philosopher to the historian, and from this cooperative activity in the course of time is formed the realistic, vigorous, and grand Weltanschauung which characterizes the intellectual work of the fully mature man. Details are lacking about the external aspect of his life at that time. From his later achievements we may conclude, however, that during the period when he taught mathematics his inclination to acquire diverse kinds of knowledge in the workshops of life—such as the study of foreign cultures, for instance—suffered no interruption. We may also conclude that, far beyond the certainty which the solution of mathematical problems affords, he was inspired by the longing and striving of mankind for the highest certainty, the rebirth of the unity of thought and feeling, of the real and the ideal, whose childhood formulations his own reflection had destroyed for him.*

* not so ill guessed!

Carlyle stayed at his teaching position in Annan for two years; then in 1816 he took a* similar position in Kirkcaldy, a village in Fifeshire,

* *etwas* [*somewhat*]. I had "*Classics*" &c as the first or chief object: Professors Leslie & Christison had recommended me.[32]

on the north of the Firth of Forth, across from Leith and Edinburgh. One of his colleagues there was Edward Irving,* who later founded the

* No, I was his "rival" rather; had been, as I found more plainly on arriving there, set up by a discontented opposition-party of his once unanimously admiring constituents; he was 3 or 4 years my senior,[33] the *facile princeps* [*indisputably first*] for success & reputation among the then Edinburgh Student[s]; famed Mathematician, &c, famed teacher (first at Haddington, then here, and *paid* beyond example, "£200 a-year," no less, with two "Assistants"[)]; a flourishing man, whom crossfortune (in the shape of myself) was beginning to nibble at! I had been rough to him, too, on the one occasion we had spoken together (had snubbed his grandiloquence to me, finding it a little *de haut en bas*, in a surly sarcastic

32. Cf. *Reminiscences*, II, 25–26.
33. For Edward Irving (1792–1834), Scottish clergyman, see *DNB* and *CL*, I, 92. Carlyle's notes to Althaus supplement his more extensive recollections of Irving in *Reminiscences*, II, 1–220.

way, which raised the laugh against him & shut him up):[34]—in spite of all which, and of my own shy ways, Irving received me with open arms; and was a brother to me, and a friend, then and elsewhere afterwards, at heart *constant* till he died. Such a friend as I never had again or before in the world. For these 3 Kirkcaldy years,[35] when we were continually together; and for the next 2? ["3" *crossed out*] while he was in Glasgow,[36] seen by me from time to time, writing to me often,—he was as the sun in my firmament, where all else had become so wintry. His talk was so genial, cordial, free-flowing, hopeful & delightful to me; all my meetings with him stand out still as sunlit. A man of noble faculties & qualities; the noblest, largest and brotherliest man, I still say, whom I have met with in my Life-journey. The sad fate he had, & how it came on him, I have marked elsewhere. His Biography is not yet known; perhaps will never be. Mrs Oliphant's Book[37] is ingenious, well-intentioned, and has a kindly, graceful and attractive quality; but her picture both of his Annan or Scottish and of his London life has little of real portraiture, and strictly speaking (except in the concluding part, where his Letters tell their own tragic, almost sacred story) is *not* to be called *like* anywhere. "Why not write his Life, yourself?" ask some. Alas, the element is *bottomless*; the labour would be great; the readers mostly questionable, many of them *bad*;—besides the ground is, for the time, in a sort preoccupied.—

Irving's influences on me were manifold; till after his removal to London, and engulfment in the mud-sea of Pulpit Popularity, we were in constant correspondence, & he knew all my secrets. Afterwards there came silence for most part, so occupied were his thoughts then; silence, but no estrangement, and broken by many a bright gleam in chance meetings. It is to him & his London journey that I owe my connexion with the Bullers, & Tutorage of the late Charles Buller; which, in all essentials, was altogether profitable & pleasant to me. Above all, it is to him, as primary

34. Cf. *Reminiscences*, II, 22–24.

35. Actually less than two: November 1816 through the summer of 1818.

36. More than three. Irving resided in Glasgow as assistant to Dr. Thomas Chalmers from October 1818 to December 1821.

37. Margaret O. W. Oliphant, *The Life of Edward Irving*, 2 vols. (London, 1862). Cf. *Reminiscences*, I, 73, 103–104; II, 216–217.

occasion (*without* which it had probably never been), that I owe *Her* and all she was to me for the last 42 years: Oh Heavens; Oh Time, oh all-engulfing Time! Irving did "introduce me to the house" at Haddington, but not while Dr Welsh lived, nor in the manner Althaus thinks.— But I must stop.[38]

Irvingite sect,[39] and since both responded to close personal relationships, it was inevitable that there would be lively discussions about religion and philosophy, the state of the world, and the needs and goals of mankind. Through Irving, Carlyle was introduced into the home of Dr. Welsh, a highly respected physician, whose daughter he married ten years later. Besides these personal relationships, the proximity of the capital was important. For with convenient connections by sea between Kirkcaldy and Leith, Edinburgh was easy to reach, and if for no other reason the wish to use the Library led him often during his vacations* over to the center

* a German notion; not fact.

of learning and of intellectual life in Scotland. Meanwhile, there seethed within him the struggle for a clearer *Weltansicht* and for the acquisition of a firm, practical point of view in the puzzling and paradoxical present in which destiny had placed him. Now and then he may well have considered seeking the peace he had lost in the service of the Church of his confined native land.* No other Church had preserved in all phases of

* never once!

life more of the puritanical severity, the unadorned rigor of faith, and the powerful religious influence of older times. On the other hand, however, nowhere did the unendurable formulas* and the dogmatic intolerance of

* write some other word;—'*formelwesen*' was not the pinching point, had there but been the preliminary of *belief* forthcoming. No Church, or speaking Entity whatever, can do without "formulas"; but it must believe them first, if it would be honest!

the Church come more harshly to light than they did when confronting the concept of freedom of thought. An independent, energetic, and

38. See *Reminiscences*, I, 146–148, and II, 85–87, for Carlyle's account of his first meeting with Jane Baillie Welsh in late May 1821. They were married in October 1826.

39. Althaus (1869) adds "He had already known Irving in Annan." Only from afar; see *Reminiscences*, II, 16–18.

freedom-loving spirit like Carlyle's was thus bound to be as repelled by these manifest shortcomings as it was shackled by certain inherent advantages. How he felt about efforts to find in the Church that peace which his own conscience had refused him, he later described trenchantly in the biography of his friend John Sterling, who succumbed to this temptation. "So dark and abstruse," he writes there,

> without lamp or authentic finger-post, is the course of pious genius towards the Eternal Kingdoms grown. No fixed highway more; the old spiritual highways and recognised paths to the Eternal, now all torn-up and flung in heaps, submerged in unutterable boiling mud-oceans of Hypocrisy and Unbelievability, of brutal living Atheism and damnable dead putrescent Cant; surely a tragic pilgrimage for all mortals; Darkness, and the mere shadow of Death, enveloping all things from pole to pole; and in the raging gulf-currents, offering us will-o'-wisps for load-stars,—intimating that there are no stars, nor ever were, except certain Old-Jew ones which have now gone out. Once more, a tragic pilgrimage for all mortals; and for the young pious soul, winged with genius, and passionately seeking land, and passionately abhorrent of floating carrion withal, more tragical than for any!—A pilgrimage we must all undertake nevertheless, and make the best of with our respective means. Some arrive; a glorious few: many must be lost,—go down upon the floating wreck which they took for land. Nay, courage! These also, so far as there was any heroism in them, have bequeathed their life as a contribution to us, have valiantly laid their bodies in the chasm for us: of these also there is no ray of heroism *lost*. . . .
>
> It is not now known, what never needed proof or statement before, that Religion is not a doubt; that it is a certainty,—or else a mockery and horror. That none or all of the many things we are in doubt about, and need to have demonstrated and rendered probable, can by any alchymy be made a 'Religion' for us; but are and must continue a baleful, quiet or unquiet, Hypocrisy for us; and bring—*salvation*, do we fancy? I think, it is another thing they will bring, and are, on all hands, visibly bringing, this good while!—[40]

But however violent may have been the torments Carlyle suffered in this surging pressure of spiritual conflict, we still hear of no attempt

40. *Life of John Sterling*, in *Works*, XI, 96–98.

to steer his course to a safe haven which did not exist for him. Uncertain as to what spiritual activity destiny had decreed for his talents, he preferred to go on patiently from day to day, awaiting the time when he might drop anchor and acknowledge that the land long sought had at last been found. He could not seriously think of another means of salvation. Even if his nature offered no guarantee against it, he found such a one in his own "Hindoo character" that was revealed in the already often cited alter ego of Professor Teufelsdröckh, in that "excellent 'Passivity' of his"[41] which was not shaken in its ideal steadfastness either by the world's opposition or by the siren song of less exalted desires. Two more years passed in this way. Carlyle was nearly twenty-three. Still wavering in his choice of career, he gave up his position at the school in Kirkcaldy about this time (late 1818*) and** accepted another

* or '19, was it? *no*, then?[42]

** '*And*' (without even a comma) this of Buller wasn't till 1822 or '23;—*and* I had, in the interim, 4 such years of solitary darkness and eating of my own heart,[43] as centuries would not make me forget.— '*Und*' indeed! A very weighty Chapter,—third or 2d Act of the whole drama,—is wanting here![44]

as tutor in Edinburgh. His pupil[45] was Charles Buller, a young man of great talent, who later was active in the Liberal party, served as chief poor law commissioner, and enjoyed the reputation of the wittiest M.P. of his day. Carlyle's efforts to obtain a position as tutor in Edinburgh were thus made under the most favorable circumstances. His relationship with Charles Buller was, however, not of long duration,[46] and a few remarks in *Sartor Resartus* lead one to conclude that his subsequent attempts in the same direction were crowned with moderate success at best.* "From private Tuition, in never so many languages and sciences,

* [*Carlyle draws a line down the margin opposite the two sentences that follow and writes:*] *Sartor* only; & refers to time anterior to Buller.

41. Harrold, *Sartor*, p. 101.
42. November 1818.
43. Beginning November 1818. Cf. note 61.
44. Cf. "The Everlasting No" of *Sartor*.
45. Changed in Althaus (1869) to "One of his pupils."
46. Thirty months. Carlyle assumed the position of tutor to Charles (1806–1848) and Arthur Buller (1808–1869) in January 1822 and resigned it in July 1824. For the Bullers, see *DNB* and *CL*, II, 4–5.

the aid derivable," he says, "is small; neither ... 'does the young Adventurer hitherto suspect in himself any literary gift; but at best earns bread-and-water wages, by his wide faculty of translation.'"[47] Translations and tutoring thus provided him a frugal living at that time. The conviction that he had a literary talent by which he could support himself was however not yet abandoned despite his wide knowledge and despite his irrepressible urge to gain a solid footing in the realm of the intellect and to create his own universe. He still wandered in the twilight, on the border between two periods of his life, and it seems that only his closer familiarity with German literature and philosophy was able to resolve his inner conflicts to a definite conclusion, set his creative powers in motion, and kindle the redeeming decision to dedicate his talents to the free humanistic activity of the mind.[48]

Already during his student years in Edinburgh his attention had been directed to German literature, specifically by Mme de Staël's *De l'Allemagne.* He got up from reading this book with the intense desire to learn German immediately in order to gain a deeper insight into the works of the great men. The French authoress had written much about their lives and activity which had awakened anxious forebodings in his soul. But interest in German literature was still so slight in England at that time that neither a German grammar nor a German tutor was to be had in Edinburgh. To be sure, Carlyle was directed, upon inquiry, to a person of whom it was said that he was a German and knew German; only upon closer examination did it turn out that this pioneer of German culture in Scotland was a "Polish Jew," or, even worse, a Jew from Courland.[49] It proved impossible even with the best of intentions to learn German from him. Carlyle was thus forced to defer his plan. His wish to become familiar with German literature continued undiminished, however, during the year which followed, when all his other reading left

47. Harrold, *Sartor*, p. 123.

48. Althaus's note: "For what follows as well as for much else in this sketch regarding the biographical details of Carlyle's life, I wish to express my gratitude to Mr. Neuberg, the translator of the *History of Frederick II* and many years a friend of Carlyle's, to whom I herewith offer my best thanks for his ready willingness to supplement and correct the very defective information which has hitherto been available in books." In Althaus (1869) the "recently deceased" Neuberg is thanked even more warmly.

49. The "Polish Jew" from Courland (or Kurland, a region now in the U.S.S.R. between the Baltic Sea and the Dvina River) was probably John Michael. See Robert Pearse Gillies, *Memoirs of a Literary Veteran* (London, 1851), II, 223.

him more or less dissatisfied. The year 1821 arrived and Carlyle, still undecided about the ultimate course his life should take, spent the winter* in his birthplace Ecclefechan.** Shortly before, one of his

* [*Carlyle corrects "winter" to "summer" and comments*:] Winter was always in Edinburgh; trying for work &c.[50]
** at Mainhill, *near* it,—a poor bare place, my Father's first Farm.

childhood friends* had returned from an extensive trip** which had

* it was at Edinburgh that the '*Jugend-freund*' of next lines first made rumour of himself, the 'wonder' &c of which is considerably overdone. His name was Jardine, Lockerby his father's abode; he had been my schoolfellow, not *class*-fellow, at Annan; a feeble enough, but a pleasant & friendly creature, with something of *skin-deep* geniality even, which marked him for 'harmless mastership in the Superficial,' amiable manners &c &c: he had attended as tutor some young Irishman (Beckwith, if I recollect, & connected with the Lockerby-House Douglases) to Göttingen; soon after this, he took orders & they gave him a Protestant Irish Living,—since which I have never heard more of him, much less seen; but remember him still with a kind of real pathos and affection.[51]

** temporary travelling tutorship.

50. I have divided Carlyle's note in two: the second part–on Robert Jardine and Carlyle's first learning of German–follows below.
51. Cf. Norton, *GC*, p. ix. What little is known of Robert Jardine of Applegarth will be found chiefly in Carlyle's note. In January 1819, while in Edinburgh for the winter, Carlyle began giving lessons in French to Jardine in return for lessons in German; with Jardine's return to his father's farm Applegarth, near Lockerbie in Annandale, in May 1819 the arrangement seems to have broken off temporarily, and Carlyle on his own began Klopstock's *Messias*. During the summer, Carlyle having returned to Mainhill where he remained until November, the lessons were resumed on a weekly basis. To his college friend John Fergusson he wrote on 25 August 1819: "The German still maintains a dubious footing; Jardine comes once a-week; but alas! he is not an Adelung; I can yet obtain only an imperfect idea of a scene in the *Misstrauische* (Distrustful), without the aid of dictionaries. Either the literature of that country little merits the praises which it has received, or my selection of German books has been singularly unfortunate. Lessing has some spirit in him; but von Cronegk and Archenholtz [*sic*] are men of mould: and Klopstock's [*sic*] Messias seems cold—dull even, if I might say so" (*CL*, I, 193). Johann Christoph Adelung (1732–1806) was a German philologist and grammarian; *Der Misstrauische* (1760) is a comedy by Johann Friedrich, Reichfreiherr Cronegk (1731–1757).

caused much stir in that part of Scotland. He had, as one said, sailed across "the eastern oceans,"* i.e., the North Sea, had been in Germany,

* oh, dear.

had lived for a while in Göttingen, and (most amazing achievement of all!) it was also rumored that he had been initiated into the mysteries of the German language. The home of this widely traveled friend who was conversant with German was now only about an hour from Ecclefechan. At a meeting in which the conversation turned upon ways the winter*

*[Carlyle crosses out "winter" and substitutes] **Summer.**

could be spent most productively, Carlyle proposed that they occupy themselves with French and German: he who knew French very well would teach it to his friend who was ignorant in this respect, while he in return was to give him the benefit of his knowledge of German. This suggestion was carried out and thus during the winter* of 1821 Carlyle

*[Carlyle crosses out "winter."]

got the first foundation of that profound knowledge of German literature which exerted such a decisive influence upon his subsequent development. Meanwhile, his widely traveled friend's knowledge of German was hardly less deplorable than the collection of books he had. Instead of the works of Goethe and Schiller, Carlyle had to be content with a few volumes of obscure dramatists of Gottsched's era, and these could hardly be suited to generate enthusiasm for German literature.[52] He was more pleased when, at his request, a Scottish sea-captain* who carried

*[Carlyle crosses out "sea-captain" and writes] **Merchant "Provost Swan" of Kirkcaldy, a very worthy & well-doing man; always a kind friend of mine.[53] I well remember the arrival of the *Schillers Werke* Sheets at Mainhill (and my impatience till the Annan Bookbinder got done with them): they had come from Lübeck, I perceived;—and except my gratitude it was needless offering Swan**

52. Such as Cronegk's *Misstrauische* and an unknown play by August von Kotzebue (1761–1819).

53. For William Swan (d. 1833), three times provost of Kirkcaldy, see *CL*, I, 143, and the anonymous life of his eldest son, also provost of Kirkcaldy, *Patrick Don Swan* (Kirkcaldy, 1893).

any attempt at payment.[54] This *Schiller*, and *Archenholz*'s 7-Years War were my first really German Books.[55]

on trade across the "eastern oceans" procured a copy of Schiller's works for him. Yet even in his first reading of Schiller he did not find that total, overpowering revelation for which his soul yearned. He now decided first and foremost to read Goethe and went to Edinburgh to fulfill that purpose.*

* 'fulfilled' that 'purpose' (somewhat gradually) *on* 'going to Edinburgh,' as he did each winter, with quite grimmer errands, not so easy of executing!

He found Goethe's works in the University Library and began with the reading of *Wilhelm Meister*. Once again it appeared at the outset that here too he would be disappointed. The farther he read, however, the more it seemed as if the scales were dropping from his eyes, and when he had finished he felt that now finally the long sought revelation would be his.*

* No, not yet;—felt only that, since the age of 15, he had read no such deep, clear, great, and widely illuminative Book;—that here, credibly and probably, *was* a man who could "reveal" to him many highest things.[56]

54. "I tell you, go on with German—" Carlyle wrote to Edward Irving on 3 June 1820. "I will lend the very best of Schiller's plays—(I have lately got them all from Ewan [Swan] of Kirkcaldy) as soon as they are bound" (*CL*, I, 255). Carlyle received through Swan Schiller's *Sämtliche Werke*, 12 vols. (Stuttgart und Tübingen, 1812–1815). Althaus in "Erinnerungen," p. 837, corrects his narrative here: he had believed the schoolfriend who taught Carlyle German to be Edward Irving.

55. Cf. Norton, *GC*, pp. ix–x. Johann Wilhelm von Archenholz (1743–1812) was a German historian and author of *Die Geschichte des Siebenjährigen Krieges*, 2 vols. (Berlin, 1793). Carlyle, who characterized Archenholz as a man "of mould" (see note 51), later recalled this history as "an old friend of mine; the first book I ever read in German" (letter to Varnhagen von Ense, 13 Nov. 1845, in *The Last Words of Thomas Carlyle* [New York: D. Appleton and Company, 1892], p. 320). For discussion of Carlyle's first acquaintance with German, see Introduction.

56. It is uncertain when Carlyle first read Goethe's *Wilhelm Meisters Lehrjahre*. Although he first refers to it by title in a letter to JWC, 26 March 1823 (*CL*, II, 316), in which he mentions a bookseller's proposal that he translate it, he had probably read it several years before. A letter of 25 September 1819 to John Fergusson, where he observes that his "unfortunate brain is entirely desiccated with the labour of reading Goethe and scratching Teutonic characters" (*CL*, I, 196), may indicate his first attempt to get through it. C. E. Norton, perhaps taking cognizance of the early date of Carlyle's reading of the *Lehrjahre* implied in Althaus's narrative, states that Carlyle must have read it before 3 June 1820, at which time he had read *Faust* (Carlyle's first reference to which is in a letter of 19 May 1820). See Sara Norton and M. A. DeWolfe

In this work poetic wealth of feeling is united with philosophical depth of thought, humanistic idealism with the active urge to a harmonious exercise of the creative powers which he had waged such long and bewildering struggles to gain. Instead of the idle brooding of the skeptic or the detached pleasure of the Epicurean gods, he heard as the epitome of all wisdom the motto "*Think of living!*"[57] and the impassioned call "*Here or nowhere is America!*"[58] About now the decision to dedicate himself completely to literary activity matured in his mind, and for nearly half a century we have seen him persevering on the path chosen at that time, and cherishing through life's storms, with undiminished zeal, the impulse toward the ideal and the sacred flame of enthusiasm from which that decision sprang.

Carlyle has repeatedly expressed in his writings his thoughts about the commitment of anyone who chooses intellectual labor as his vocation. His view was the same as that which Fichte set forth in his lectures "On the Nature of the Scholar." What drew him to our great classical writers was chiefly the depth of idealism—that heroic unity of life and work—in which the roots of their true greatness lay. He believed, with Fichte, that all things which we see or work with are a kind of garment or sense impression under which, as its essence, lies hidden "the Divine Idea of the World."[59] No such divine idea of the world is perceptible to most persons. They live merely amid surface appearances, without dreaming of the divine idea that lies underneath. But the writer is sent here especially to recognize this divine idea and to reveal it to us. Since in each new generation it will manifest itself in new terms, he exists to serve as

Howe, *The Letters of Charles Eliot Norton* (Boston and New York: Houghton Mifflin, 1913), I, 481–482; cf. Norton, *GC*, p. xiv, and *Works*, XXVII, 8. Carlyle does not seem to have read it carefully until 1821 and not until late 1823 and early 1824 did he translate it from the 1816 Berlin edition which he eventually owned. Many references to Goethe's novel in these years and later reveal the exceptional stature he accorded it. See *CL*, III, 260, *Reminiscences*, II, 115, and Arthur A. Adrian, "Dean Stanley's Report of Conversations with Carlyle," *Victorian Studies*, 1 (Sept. 1957), 74. The last-cited appears to confirm that the book mentioned in the letter to John Fergusson of 25 September 1819 was indeed the *Lehrjahre*.

57. See *Works*, XXIV, 120. Cf. *Works*, XXVII, 373, and *Two Note Books* (New York: Grolier Club, 1898), p. 278.

58. See *Works*, XXIX, 11. Cf. Harrold, *Sartor*, pp. 196–197.

59. Many times throughout life Carlyle recalled with reverence this concept from Fichte's "Über das Wesen des Gelehrten." See especially "Characteristics" in *Works*, XXVIII, 31, and *On Heroes, Hero-Worship, & the Heroic in History* in *Works*, V, 156. Carlyle takes up Fichte in the seminal essay of 1827 "State of German Literature" in *Works*, XXVI; see particularly p. 59, and cf. *CL*, IV, 271–272.

its spokesman. For this reason the writer is both the prophet and the priest who proclaims the divine to man. With his fellows he belongs to a great priesthood which over the centuries has taught all men that a god is still present in their lives and that all appearance which we see in this world is nothing more than a garment of the divine idea which lies hidden under the surface of appearances. "Of all Priesthoods, Aristocracies, Governing Classes at present extant in the world," he cries out elsewhere, "there is no class comparable for importance to that Priesthood of the Writers of Books. . . . The writers of Newspapers, Pamphlets . . . Books, these *are* the real working effective Church of a modern country. . . . The Writer of a Book, is not he a Preacher preaching not to this parish or that, on this day or that, but to all men in all times and places?"[60]

Carlyle began his literary work in the spirit of a prophetic and priestly mission, created by our great poets and thinkers and confirmed by his own innermost nature. The key to his nature and to his intellectual work lies in understanding his desire to present in suitable form the contrast, shining forth in a thousand shapes and colors, between "the Divine Idea" and the passing appearances; to justify that idea, as seen in the religious endeavor and in all walks of life, as the true and essential as opposed to the appearances, as seen in the changing and the inadequate; and to do all this with the religious conviction of a priest and the sorrowful lamentation of a prophet. Perhaps never before the "writer" Thomas Carlyle has there been a transcendental thinker who in his bold flights of speculation brought such passionate devotion to resolving the practical problems of the contemporary world.

When after such long hesitation he finally took the step, however, there still remained much to do before the elements which had been stirred up could come to rest. He had the will and the enthusiasm for a definite labor. However, the field was large, the choice difficult, and the ranks of colleagues among whom he had to find a place were already crowded. Thus it was all the more important to make a start since literary work was not merely to be the means of realizing his inner calling but was also to serve as the basis of an independent existence. Journalism* offered the

* Never thought of, or had the least to do with any branch of that!—

---

60. *Works*, V, 168, 162, 159. Althaus's analysis of Fichte's ideas closely follows Carlyle's. See especially pp. 156–158.

best chance of combining both goals, and it was as a journalist that Carlyle began his new career. Edinburgh then enjoyed an exciting intellectual life. The genius of Robert Burns had* aroused the poetic sense of

* ach!

the Scots; Sir Walter Scott's fame was at its height; there was no lack of distinguished persons in the sciences; and the *Edinburgh Review* formed the center of a circle of talented writers whose work already enjoyed influence and respect beyond the borders of England. Allusions in *Sartor Resartus* indicate* that previous to this time Carlyle had attracted

* *totally* fictitious!

attention in Edinburgh literary circles as a man of intellect and originality. That he now settled there to enter unaided the ranks of the literary community suggests that he overcame his innate disposition toward solitude* and frequented these circles often. His first writings to become

* alas! He had no such "*Hang*" [*disposition*], it was a force laid on him.— All this is *wrong*, but can be corrected from the opposite leaf.

All this is a coil of mistakes; chronologically & otherwise, quite wrong. I never dreamed of '*Journalistik*' [*journalism*], was entirely unknown in 'Edinburgh circles'; solitary, "eating my own heart,"[61] fast losing my health, too; a prey, in fact, to nameless struggles and miseries, which have yet a kind of horror in them to my thought.[62] Three weeks without *any* Sleep (from *im*possibility to be free of noise), &c &c.[63] The 'Articles' mentioned below were all written during this *Ante*-Buller period; to help my poor economics a little (*capital* brought from Kirkcaldy, perhaps about £80 or £90, could never be brought to *increase* considerably, & was sometimes-half way *done*),—the advent of Buller first set *finance* on a firm basis, and I *ceased* my 'Articles.' I had spent the winters in Edinburgh, 'looking out for employment' on those dismal terms; the summers (had it only been for cheapness' sake) at my Father's.

61. "*Cor ne edito*; Eat not the heart," in Bacon's "Of Friendship." The metaphor goes back to Pythagoras. See C. E. Norton's excellent note in his edition of *Two Note Books of Thomas Carlyle* (New York: Grolier Club, 1898), p. 165.
62. Cf. Froude, *Carlyle*, I, 98.
63. Cf. ibid., p. 64.

Nothing in "*Sartor*" thereabouts[64] is *fact* (symbolical *myth* all) except that of the "*incident* in the Rue St Thomas de l'Enfer,"— which occurred quite literally to myself in Lieth [*Leith*] Walk, during those 3 weeks of total sleeplessness, in which almost my one solace was that of a daily bathe on the sands between Lieth and Portobello. Incident was as I went *down* (coming *up* I generally felt a little refreshed for the hour); I remember it well, & could go yet to about the place.— *Legendre's Geometry* was done in the name of Brewster; and, I think, had not been got quite finished, when my Tutorship of Charles Buller commenced (£200 a-year &c &c).[65] I remember doing the *Essay on Proportion*,—one Sunday forenoon; thought ["& think" *crossed out*] it rather *good*, and have never seen it since.[66] One year (perhaps the 2*d* or 3*d* before) I had

---

64. A. Carlyle notes that "thereabouts" is omitted by Froude, who publishes part of this long passage in *Carlyle*, I, 101. Since Carlyle's note refers specifically to the climactic moment of Teufelsdröckh's despair in "The Everlasting No" (Harrold, *Sartor*, pp. 166–168), Froude's omission of "thereabouts" significantly alters the sense of the passage. "It does not follow," A. Carlyle perceptively observes, "that because the work is mythical 'here' or 'thereabouts' (i.e. in one or two specified passages) it is mythical throughout" (NLS: MS 1800; cf. *LL*, II, 365–366). He convincingly places Carlyle's conversion, set by Froude in June 1821, in July or early August 1821 or, more likely, 1822 (see *LL*, II, 380–382). This latter date, which the notes to Althaus confirm, is generally accepted today. The improvement in Carlyle's mental state came about through a number of causes. These include his first meeting with Jane Baillie Welsh late in May 1821 and the generally favorable progress of his largely epistolary courtship of her; his first thorough reading sometime in 1821 of *Wilhelm Meisters Lehrjahre*, which proved a revelation to him; his engagement as tutor for Charles and Arthur Buller in January 1822, which provided a measure of financial stability; his growing realization that literature was to be his life's work; and of course his gradually improving health. Froude, by placing the conversion in June 1821, the time Carlyle first met Miss Welsh, implies (though never explicitly states) that she had more to do with it than she actually did. That it was not as abrupt as in *Sartor* and that his recovery extended over many years is the argument of two important articles by Carlisle Moore, "*Sartor Resartus* and the Problem of Carlyle's 'Conversion,'" *PMLA*, 70 (Sept. 1955), 662–681, and "The Persistence of Carlyle's 'Everlasting Yea,'" *Modern Philology*, 54 (Feb. 1957), 187–196. It receives explicit corroboration from several of Carlyle's other notes to Althaus. On the conversion, see also *Reminiscences*, II, 180; Harrold, *CGT*, pp. 41–44.

65. January 1822.

66. Carlyle's translation of Adrien Marie Legendre's *Elements of Geometry and Trigonometry; with Notes and Additions, and an Introductory Chapter on Proportion* appeared in 1824; the title page has David Brewster as editor. He had begun the translation in December 1821 and, with some aid from his brother John, worked on it from April to July 1822. He met Legendre briefly in Paris in 1824.

thought of attempting to become an advocate (seemed glorious to me for its "independency" &c); & I did read some Law-Books, and attend (Hume's) *Lectures on Scots Law*, and converse with and question various dull people, of the "practical" sort; but *it*, & they, and the admired Lecturer Baron Hume himself (*David*'s Nephew)[67] appeared to me mere denizens of the Kingdom of Dulness, pointing towards nothing but money &c as wages for all that bog-pool of disgusts; Hume's *Lectures* once done with, I flung the thing away forever.[68] Tait (and I think hardly any other Bookseller) I tried with various Literary Projects (no Ms.-'Book' of my own, but merely to edit, translate &c): one and all, rejected without a discussion. I had no friend to consult & commune with; perhaps twice in the week or so, some weak acquaintance to walk; —except, now & then, with Irving for a day or two, I was *solus*, wandering as in endless labyrinths, flinty, muddy, thorny, under a sky all *leaden.*—[69] Enough of that: here is my *guess* at the *Chronologies* of this 'second or third act' of poor life-drama now verging towards 'end of 5th'!—

Quit Kirkcaldy, 1819 (*beginning* or *end*, I cannot now say *which*);[70] I well see myself yet, stepping up by the Old Theatre, in a dirty wet wintry afternoon, with the feeling in me, "Kirk is over the horizon to me; Schoolmastering ditto next (better *die* than be a Schoolmaster for one's living)[71] —*possible*, surely, to find *something* other that will give honest wages if one do it honestly!"—*this* feeling, in very bad spirits (for *dyspepsia* already had me secretly by the throat), & that there was something of "1819" in my head withal: but farther I cannot recollect.[72]

Try Scots Law; write (pitifully enough) 'Articles' (as said was) Brewsters *Encyclopedia*;[73] fight with the dismallest Lernean Hydra

67. David Hume (1757–1838), nephew of the philosopher and historian. Carlyle began attending Hume's lectures on Scots law in November 1819 but gradually lost interest and had abandoned the subject by spring 1820. Lockhart in *The Life of Sir Walter Scott* (Edinburgh: Robert Cadell, 1842), p. 17, records Scott's altogether more favorable impression of Hume's lectures.
68. Cf. Froude, *Carlyle*, I, 64.
69. Cf. A. Carlyle, *LL*, II, 380–381.
70. November 1818.
71. Cf. Froude, *Carlyle*, I, 55.
72. Carlyle usually speaks of his illnesses as beginning in 1818.
73. Seventeen of Carlyle's twenty articles for David Brewster's *Edinburgh Encyclo-*

of problems,[74] spiritual, temporal, eternal;—"eat my own heart";[75] but authentically take the Devil by the nose withal[76] (see 'incident in Rue St Thomas'), and fling *him* behind me, 1820, '21, '22;[77] till *Legendre* &c with *rather* improving prospect of wages; and finally on Irving's call to London, Charles Buller arrives, summer of 1823, and pressure of finance as good as disappears for the time. (I was always capable of strict frugality; never was *in debt* in my life).[78]— — In 1822, it must have been, that I first went to Haddington, and made the most important acquaintance that has happened in my history!—[79] Twice or thrice, in Irving's time, I went visiting to Glasgow for a few days; & saw a much more *fertile* kind of people: Glasgow Merchants one or two,[80] Carl*i*les of Paisley (kinsmen after a sort),[81] William Graham of Burnswark[82] &c;—and was rather cheered by the evidently good impression I made on all of them. In Edinburgh from my fellow creatures little or nothing but *vinegar* was my reception— cup [*i.e., a slight bow*] when we happened to meet or pass near each other;—my own blame mainly, so proud, shy, poor, at

---

paedia were reprinted in *Montaigne and Other Essays*, ed. S. R. Crockett (London: James Gowans & Son, 1897); A. Carlyle added the eighteenth, in *LL*, I, 268, and G. B. Tennyson the final two, in "Unnoted Encyclopaedia Articles by Carlyle," *English Language Notes*, 1 (Dec. 1963), 108–112. See also *CL*, I, 259–260n. "The period of his most intense activity on behalf of the *Encyclopaedia*" was "from 1819 to mid-1821, after which time Carlyle no longer mentions any encyclopaedia articles by name" (Tennyson, *Sartor*, p. 341). A few he may have written in 1822 and 1823.

74. Poisonous many-headed water-snake that lived in the marshes of Lerna, near Argos in Greece. When one head was cut off, others grew in its place. Hercules slew it as his second labor.

75. See note 61.

76. Cf. Froude, *Carlyle*, I, 78, who substitutes "horns" for "nose."

77. Cf. Froude, *Carlyle*, I, 64, when he speaks of Carlyle entering "the three most miserable years of my life."

78. On a few occasions Carlyle borrowed money but always repaid it promptly, e.g., in July 1831 he accepted a loan of £60 from Jeffrey.

79. See note 38.

80. David Hope (d. 1857) principally, a close friend of Irving's. See *Reminiscences*, II, 10, 71, 77–78.

81. Chiefly Warrand Carlile (1796–1893), who married Agnes ("Nancy"), Irving's youngest sister, in 1820.

82. William Graham (1770–after 1853), who was born in Burnswark (three miles north of Carlyle's birthplace in Ecclefechan) and returned there in 1823 after the collapse of his business in Glasgow. See *CL*, I, 274, and *Reminiscences*, II, 71, 78–84.

once so insignificant-looking and so grim and sorrowful. That in *Sartor*, of the '*worm* trodden & proving a *torpedo*, and sending you ceiling-high to be borne home on shutters' is not wholly a fable; but did actually befal once or twice, as I still (with a kind of small not ungenial malice) can remember.[83] [Probably, nay I now think almost certainly it must have been in 1822;—1818 the retreat from Kirkcaldy? It could be settled from my *Letters*;— but worth my while or *not*? I will *proceed* on that hypothesis of 1822.][84]

Autumn 1822 the Buller Family comes (only Charles & Brother till that): they like me well; good people both; *Lady* very clever, witty &c, but of Calcutta *genus*, light as gossamer, full of whims, changes:[85] all winter & next spring, I continue in my *Lodgings*; very *sick*, dyspeptic, shiveringly sensible to *noises*, sleepless &c &c. Summer 1823 we all shift to *Kinnaird* House (in sight of Killiecrankie, across river; ride thither once); am writing *Schiller* for *London Magazine* (Edward Irving had put me on it,—sight of him on his 'wedding Jaunt,' in the highest feather, that summer); very miserable from ill-health.[86] Summer of 1824, my *Meister* had come out; Buller Family all to London; I follow in Lieth *Smack*. Change of plan, by Mrs B.; change *on* change &c &c; I, sickly in the extreme, *give up*; Charles goes to Cambridge &c; I to Lodgings, to Badams of Birmingham;[87] to Dover, to Paris (for a week or so)— decide, at last (for neither Badam's fine *ridings* nor any recipe would relieve my bitter *bodily* miseries), to complete *Schiller* as a *Book*, then go *home*, get a *House* there of my own, *quiet* at last. 1825, early spring, settle at *Hoddam*-Hill (pretty little farm of one's own!) *German Romance* done mostly there; *legal* hurlyburlies end the 'farm'; *quit* (May 26) 1826, and move to Scotsbrig, as the *Mainhill*ites were all doing,—having openly broken with their unjust *high*-riding Landlord[88] (on *my* score & *Hoddam* Hill's),—

83. Harrold, *Sartor*, p. 129. Cf. Froude, *Carlyle*, I, 57.

84. Carlyle's brackets.

85. For Charles Buller (1774–1848), a retired Anglo-Indian judge, and his wife (d. 1848), see *CL*, II, 4–5.

86. Cf. *Reminiscences*, II, 109–113.

87. For John Badams (d. 1833) of Birmingham, see *CL*, III, 94–95, and *Reminiscences*, I, 93, and II, 134, 144–148.

88. General Matthew Sharpe (d. 1845), the Carlyle family's landlord at Mainhill and Hoddam Hill. Carlyle narrates the incident more fully in *Reminiscences*, I, 49–50, and *CL*, IV, 142–143. For his expanded account of his life from 1824 to 1826, see *Reminiscences*, II, 113–181.

where they still continue, my youngest Brother now alone left of them. At Scotsbrig (happy in my riding-horses, & in every sort of kindness & affection, my *spiritual* struggles now become victorious, too),[89] I continue till *German Romance* get out; and in Autumn 1826 (very poor, very *road*less, unconnected in the world, and still very dyspeptic,—these being my *only*, but sufficient sources of chagrin), I venture on wedding, on taking with me the brightest and bravest little Female Soul, upon such a Pilgrimage as there seldom was for such; & we settle in a small neat house in Comley Bank, Edinburgh, all standing ready for us,—and are as lonely as two wood-doves in their nest for the first year or so; very lonely, and with outlooks very bad, had not *we*, and especially *she*, stood true to them and one another. Oh my Loved One, oh my Jeannie!—

We went to Craigenputtoch, May 1828, as to the *cheaper* & healthier, and advisable kind of place; for we were poor enough; and had made no Conquest in Edinburgh,—except that of Jeffrey (which was very bright to us for some years), and thereby of occasional admittance to his *Review*, and to the *Foreign* or *Foreign Quarterly* in consequence. Edinburgh Review of *Jean Paul* and in next Number *State of German Literature* for the first time brought my name out,—& this with wonder in great deal rather than admiration *any*.[90]

known were articles on Montesquieu, Montaigne, Nelson and the two Pitts in Brewster's *Edinburgh Encyclopaedia*,[91] together with a translation of Legendre's *Elements of Geometry*, published the same year (1823) with an appended "Essay on Proportion." These were first efforts which Carlyle later judged unworthy to be included in his collected *Miscellanies* and for which mere chronological mention suffices here. The real beginning of a significant and strictly defined period of his literary activity dates only from 1824, when he brought out his edition of Goethe's *Wilhelm Meister*. About this time he had evidently come to a decision about his future course of study and work. His studies focused primarily on German

89. See Carlisle Moore's two articles cited in note 64, Harrold, *Sartor*, p. 198, and *Reminiscences*, II, 177–181.

90. Carlyle writes at greater length of his marriage, his life at Comley Bank (the usual spelling) in Edinburgh, his removal to Craigenputtoch, and his association with Jeffrey and the *Edinburgh Review* in *Reminiscences*, chiefly I, 80–91, 96–98, and II, 235–252.

91. See note 73.

literature, and his first task was to impart the results of these studies to his countrymen. As he explained in the preface to his translation of *Wilhelm Meister*, German literature was practically unknown in England.[92] People had a dim notion that over the last hundred years Germany had produced a number of poets of no mean reputation. Mention the names Klopstock, Wieland, Goethe and Schiller, and here and there a few people would have read one or another of their works in bad translations. The general recognition of their achievements was, however, thoroughly inadequate, and the prevailing attitude was that in true poetry and culture, as in the development of her social and political institutions, Germany still lagged very far behind other countries. From his reading of German works Carlyle had developed a completely different view. To him they had offered a new revelation, and the direction of his studies was determined as much by the irresistible need to immerse himself in this newly discovered intellectual world and to cultivate from it his inner self, as it was by the wish to make its riches available to his countrymen. In its external lines, one would designate this period of Carlyle's life, devoted almost exclusively to exploring and working with German literature, as spanning the years from 1824 to 1833; in its inner workings, it exerted, as was observed above, a lasting influence upon Carlyle's whole being and thought. However varied the matter upon which he would later try his strength and however rugged and splendid an independence his intellectual individuality would develop, he rested solidly upon the foundation laid at that time. The echo of German poetry and philosophy is unmistakable in the form and content of all his works.

The translation of *Wilhelm Meister* was excellent*—obviously a work

* **no, it was baddish in parts—I tried to help it** *afterwards*.[93]

of reverence and love, the most faithful translation into a foreign tongue of Goethe's wonderful work. To the superficial and dogmatic critics of German literature in England—of whom the most prominent were Jeffrey, the editor of the *Edinburgh Review*, and De Quincey the Opium-

92. *Works*, XXIII, 3–5.

93. See the preface to the second edition of *Wilhelm Meister's Apprenticeship* and *Wilhelm Meister's Travels*, published together by James Fraser in 1839, in *Works*, XXIII, 1. De Quincey pointed out a few of the Scotticisms and infelicities in Carlyle's translation of the *Apprenticeship* in the *London Magazine*, 10 (Aug. 1824), 189–197, and (Sept. 1824), 291–307. Carlyle admits to the justice of some of De Quincey's criticisms in *CL*, III, 174–175, 260, and in *Reminiscences*, II, 151–152.

eater—it offered nothing more, however, than a new opportunity to display once again their narrow-minded, anti-German rhetoric.[94] Carlyle viewed Goethe as the man who described and presented human affairs with poetic genius. These critics tried to make him into the "dandy" of the era of George IV, the man of high society, of fashionable dress, and of conventional respectability—and one can hardly be surprised that they were disappointed. German literature, they said, oscillated between two evils: bad taste on the one hand, mysticism on the other.[95] From one point of view, the prevailing mores of Germany exclude the middle-class poet and scholar from the circles of high society, while from another the poverty in which he is assumed to live makes him languish in wretched and mean circumstances. No other outcome is possible until such time as a fundamental revolution in this state of affairs takes place. That was in substance the judgment of the critics, and the huge gap which separates the thinker longing for truth and beauty from the sophisticated men of the world divided Carlyle from them. He too was poor and, like those impoverished German writers and scholars, had to struggle for his daily bread. He had long ago made his choice between the quest for the material and that for the spiritual, between the appreciation which the temper of the times afforded and that which his own consciousness allowed him. Disparaging comments could neither shake him in his faith nor turn him away from the loving exploration of the riches which German literature and philosophy had revealed to him. From the study of Goethe he turned next to the study of Schiller, and already in 1824* there

* [*Carlyle crosses out "4" and substitutes*] 5.

appeared—as the first independent work of his literary endeavors—his *Life of Schiller*. In light of the aforementioned attitude toward German literature, the Edinburgh publishers* might well be apprehensive over

* **never had heard of it, they—**

94. Jeffrey's notice of *Wilhelm Meister's Apprenticeship* was published in the *Edinburgh Review*, 42 (Aug. 1825), 409–449; see especially pp. 409–417. See also De Quincey's review (cited in the previous note), especially pp. 189, 190, 303.

95. Jeffrey's criticism, pp. 417–418 of his review. For Carlyle's opinion of this review see *CL*, III, 400 and cf. *Works*, XXVII, 134. He in effect replies to it and defends the Germans against the charges of bad taste and mysticism in his "State of German Literature," *Works*, XXVI, 26–86, especially p. 37ff. and p. 70ff.

the dubious venture of sponsoring this new tribute to the German genius. Actually, the *Life of Schiller* came out, not in Edinburgh, but in the pages of the *London Magazine*, which was at the time edited by Charles Lamb.*

* *Ach Gott!*[96]

In the following* year Carlyle made his first trip to London and there

*[*Carlyle crosses out "following," substitutes*] current [*and inserts after "year"*] (1824).

found* a publisher who, upon completion of serial publication in the

*[*Carlyle crosses out "found" and corrects it to*] had found.

*London,** published the work as a book. It appeared anonymously, as did

* whose editor '*Verleger*' [*the publisher*] was,

all of Carlyle's works until 1837, made its mark however, and even now, after all that has since been written on Schiller, must bear comparison with the best biographies of the poet which we have.* Full and accurate

* it is a very poor work; written mostly at Kinnaird in Perthshire; in the silence of the little *old* House there, begirt with woods, with solitude, pain and melancholy. *New* 'House,' (where *Buller Family* sat in such hours), is a 300 yards off: in the evenings (except Sunday), I wasn't there.[97]

in its facts, imaginative and comprehensive in its portrayal, thorough and well-informed in its evaluation, it combines these qualities with a warm understanding of human character and a profound insight into the evolution and the ideal of mankind and the writer. This gives the literary work its true inspiration and at the same time satisfies aesthetically the moral vigor of the mind. Facts he was able to draw from outside sources, but the heroic interpretation of Schiller's character and life (an interpretation

96. Althaus confuses the point. The editors and publishers of the *London Magazine* were John Taylor and James Hessey. Lamb, a leading contributor, first published his *Essays of Elia* in the *London*'s pages. Carlyle's "Schiller's Life and Writings" appeared in the October 1823, January 1824, and the July through September 1824 numbers; Taylor & Hessey republished it in volume form as *The Life of Friedrich Schiller* in 1825. Carlyle thought little of Lamb and drew many satiric pen portraits of him.

97. Cf. *Reminiscences*, II, 113–114, and *Early Letters of Thomas Carlyle*, ed. C. E. Norton (London: Macmillan, 1886), I, 201.

frequently recalling Wilhelm von Humboldt's superb characterization published five years later[98]) is his very own, and recognition of this was accorded him even in Germany where the work became known soon after its appearance. "Of this biography of Schiller," Goethe wrote in a short notice, "one can say only the best. It is remarkable because it reveals a careful study of the events in the life of our poet as well as a study of the writings of our friend, and a personal identification with them inevitably emerges. It is extraordinary how the biographer provides a satisfying insight into the character and the great merit of the man, and he does this with a clarity and discretion that was hardly to have been expected from someone so far away."[99] Such encouraging praise from a man of Goethe's stature could well console Carlyle for much misunderstanding. This was certainly the case when, during the year (1826) following the publication of the *Life of Schiller*, he sent Goethe a copy of his translation of *Wilhelm Meister*, and the correspondence between the two men (to which we shall soon return) began.[100] It hardly needs saying that it reinforced in no small measure Carlyle's predilection for German studies.

Carlyle had meanwhile* returned to Edinburgh and immersed himself

* Not at all; returned to Annandale; wedded in 1826; and then, but not till then.

deeper than ever in German literature and philosophy. A long pause*

* [*Carlyle crosses out "A long" and writes*] no pause at all; was doing *German Romance*, steadily as an 8-day clock, & silently gathering some health, not to speak of perfect deliverance to the poor doubting soul of him.[101]

98. *Briefwechsel zwischen Schiller und W. von Humboldt (in den Jahren 1792 bis 1805). Mit einer Vorerinnerung über Schiller und den Gang seiner Geistesentwicklung* (Stuttgart und Tübingen, 1830).

99. *Goethes Werke* (Weimar, 1903), XLI, 302 (my translation). See also Carlyle's *Works*, XXV, 322–345. The German edition with Goethe's preface appeared in 1830.

100. Carlyle first wrote to Goethe in 1824, but a regular interchange of letters began only in 1827.

101. Cf. *Reminiscences*, II, 179–180, and *CL*, IV, 142. Carlyle's certainty in speaking of the "perfect deliverance to the poor doubting soul of him" implies a more absolute resolution of the 1822 Leith Walk conversion than Carlisle Moore contends in his two articles cited in note 64. Cf. Froude, *Carlyle*, I, 330: "First battle won in the Rue de l'Enfer—Leith Walk—four years before. Campaign not ended till now [1825–1826]."

apparently occurred in his literary endeavors; in any event his collected works have no work dated 1826. In the meantime, the two years which followed show him nonetheless eagerly stepping forth in various directions, acquiring knowledge, and reflecting. Above all, we must note that it was about now that he became acquainted with the works of Jean Paul, the German writer whose style and way of thinking unquestionably exerted the greatest influence upon him, an influence recognizable even in his most recent works and by means of which many of his literary characteristics and idiosyncrasies may be explained.* It is not that we wish to

* Yes; translating of his *Quintus Fixlein* first taught me to *read* him fairly;[102] perhaps it was little De Quincey's reported admiration ("Goethe a mere *corrupted* pigmy to him" &c)[103] that first put me upon trying to be orthodox and admire. I dimly felt poor De Quincey (who then passed for a mighty seer in such things) to have exaggerated, and to know perhaps but little of either Jean Paul or Goethe (which was the fact); however, I held on, reading and considerably ["partly" *crossed out*] admiring Jean Paul, on my own score, tho' always with something of (secret) disappointment. Should now *wish*, perhaps, that I hadn't?— My *first* favourite Books had been *Hudibras* & *Tristram Shandy*; everybody was proclaiming it such a feat for a man, "To have wit, to have humour"[104] above all! There was always a small secret something of *affectation*, which is now not secret to me, in that part of my affairs.[105]

present Jean Paul as Carlyle's model or Carlyle as Jean Paul's imitator. It goes without saying that such a lasting and extraordinary effect of the one upon the other could not have occurred without the existence of kindred temperaments or without the possession of creative powers which were deeply rooted in personalities of similar orientations and which

102. Carlyle translated Richter's *Life of Quintus Fixlein* for his *German Romance* in 1826.

103. Carlyle seems to be loosely remembering De Quincey's article "Jean Paul Frederick Richter" in the *London Magazine*, 4 (Dec. 1821), 606–612, where De Quincey praised Jean Paul at the expense of Goethe. De Quincey continued his attack on Goethe in his two-part notice of Carlyle's translation of *Wilhelm Meisters Lehrjahre* cited in note 93.

104. Perhaps an echo of Pope, "Epistle to Miss Blount," l. 27: "Have Humour, Wit, a native Ease and Grace."

105. Cf. Froude, *Carlyle*, I, 396–397.

responded to comparable impulses. Jean Paul, transposed into nineteenth-century England and Scotland, would have perhaps been a Carlyle; Carlyle, transposed into eighteenth-century Germany, perhaps a Jean Paul.* Both had in common unbounded poetic intuition and imagination,

* Never, I should think, in any conceivable case. Jean Paul and I are not made alike, but differently *very*.

both had the desire always to know more, both had the visionary humanitarian idealism; in both, finally, the impact of this idealism matured amid the circumstances of the real world into the intellectual flowering of a temperament embracing tears and laughter. But however much they had in common, their differences remain just as unmistakable; and as strikingly as Carlyle reminds one in many ways of Jean Paul, just as little does this affect the independence of his literary character. He had a more austere nature than Jean Paul. With all its idealism his mind was drawn more to real life and to history; his humor, in the last analysis, was supported more by a deep Dantesque melancholy than by the effusive sentimentality of his German predecessor.* One wonders, however,

* That is true.

whether Carlyle's writings would have had, without his knowledge of Jean Paul, the singular form and diction which gives them so exceptional a place in English literature. The transformation from the pure, powerful, measured style of his first works to the Germanized, Jean-Paulized exposition of his later period must always be regarded as an extraordinary phenomenon.*

* Edward Irving and his admiration of the Old Puritans & Elizabethans (whom, at heart, I never could entirely adore, tho' trying hard), his and everybody's doctrine on that head, played a much more important part than Jean Paul on my poor "style";— & the most important part by far was that of Nature, you would perhaps say, had you ever heard my Father speak, or very often heard my Mother & her inborn melodies of heart and of voice![106]

106. Cf. Froude, *Carlyle*, I, 397, and, for Carlyle on his father's style of speaking, *Reminiscences*, I, 5. Cf. also *Reminiscences*, II, 41, where Carlyle, speaking of Irving, writes: "He affected the Miltonic or Old-English Puritan style, and strove visibly to imitate it more and more, till almost the end of his career, when indeed it had become his own, and was the language he used in utmost heat of business, for expressing his

Besides, he did not by any means limit his studies to the works of Jean Paul. He also read Klopstock and the Saxon writers Winckelmann and Lessing; the writers of the Göttingen group Tieck, Novalis and the two Schlegels; Kant, Fichte and Schelling. In short, he went thoroughly into German literature and philosophy of the eighteenth and nineteenth centuries, in a way that no one of his countrymen, then or before, ever had. The viewpoint from which he considered this wealth of intellectual works did not exclude a single one of the major criteria upon which a writer's total significance depends: it combined the historical and the aesthetic with the moral and the intellectual, and though he valued most the last two, he never lost sight of the claims of the others. These great men he regarded as his comrades in the universal human struggle for the true, the good, and the beautiful.[107] From revelations of their spiritual nature his sympathies instinctively flowed over to their personal destinies within the historical epochs, and the social conditions in which fate had placed them. Similarly, his aesthetic credo centered itself on the ancient Greek concept of the καλοκἀγαθον—the unity of the good and the beautiful. However, he did not restrict this concept to the realm of art but applied it also to what he observed in all provinces of life, as symbolic of the supreme harmony of all humanity: the unity of thought and action, of imagination and reality. The lively stimulation which these German studies must have offered one with such a turn of mind as his needs no explanation. It was in character, however, that in fact no philosopher attracted him with greater force than Fichte: Fichte, the man of energetic, turbulent, unbending personality; Fichte, the bold thinker, who not only

---

meaning. . . . To his example also, I suppose, I owe something of my own poor affectations in that matter, which are now more or less visible to me, much repented of or not. We were all taught at that time, by Coleridge etc., that the old English Dramatists, Divines, Philosophers, judicious Hooker, Milton, Sir Thomas Browne, were the genuine exemplars; which I also tried to believe, but never rightly could *as a whole*. . . ." Froude, basing his opinion on Carlyle's note to Althaus, denied emphatically that Carlyle's style was founded on Jean Paul's (*Carlyle*, I, 396). Sterling, in his study of Carlyle's achievement (*London and Westminster Review*, 33 [Oct. 1839], 1–68), comments incisively on Jean Paul's influence on Carlyle (see especially pp. 9–11). Althaus is indebted to this discussion.

107. Althaus alludes to the last two lines of the fifth stanza of Goethe's poem "Generalbeichte" (1804): "Und in Ganzen, Guten, Schönen, / Resolut zu leben" (*Goethes Werke* [Weimar, 1887], I, 127). Carlyle often quoted Goethe's lines, usually (and significantly) substituting "the True" for "the Beautiful." See, for example, *Works*, XXVII, 173 and 384.

constructed his system of transcendental idealism with rigorous consistency but who also came down from the world of the imagination into the world of reality and there took the measure of his own age against the standard of the presumed wants and goals of mankind. One can indeed say that here too Carlyle had encountered a kindred spirit, and even in his later years he often preferred to return to the well-known works of the man whose philosophical system corresponded in most respects to the principles upon which he based his own intellectual outlook.

The next results of his studies were two articles in the *Edinburgh Review*—one on Jean Paul, the other on the "State of German Literature" in general—together with* four volumes of translations from Goethe, Jean

* No, not *nebst* [*together with*], these [*i.e., the four volumes of* German Romance] do bear date 1827 on Titlepage; but they had been finished, and paid for, the Autumn before: the poor scrubby payment (£180 or so) was part of my marriage outfit, as I well remember. These translations are good, and I could not do better yet; but nobody took the least notice of them, I believe; two Books of somewhat similar titles, by a couple of silly enough fellows, happened to come out about the same time, and absorbed any attention there was.—[108]

Paul, Tieck, Musäus and Hoffmann entitled *German Romance*—all published in 1827. From his excellent article on Jean Paul, a few passages (given here) perhaps best shed light on Carlyle's opinion of him, what he admired, what he took exception to, and in what a remarkable way not only the censure but also the admiration bear upon many traits in his own character. "Richter," Carlyle said,

> has been called an intellectual Colossus; and in truth it is somewhat in this light that we view him. His faculties are all of gigantic mould; cumbrous, awkward in their movements; large and splendid, rather than harmonious or beautiful; yet joined in living union; and of force and compass altogether extraordinary. He has an intellect vehement, rugged, irresistible; crushing in pieces the hardest

108. Thomas Roscoe, *German Novelists*, 4 vols. (1826), and Robert Pearse Gillies, *German Stories . . .* (1826). A few years before had appeared Edgar Taylor, *German Popular Stories . . .* (1823), illustrated by George Cruikshank. Writing to a friend in 1826 Carlyle thought his "poor Book, however . . . to a great degree uninterfered with by any of these Works" (*CL*, IV, 162).

problems; piercing into the most hidden combinations of things, and grasping the most distant: an imagination vague, sombre, splendid, or appalling; brooding over the abysses of Being; wandering through Infinitude, and summoning before us, in its dim religious light, shapes of brilliancy, solemnity, or terror*: a fancy of exuber-

* not very *exact*, this!

ance literally unexampled; for it pours its treasures with a lavishness which knows no limit. . . . But deeper than all these lies Humour, the ruling quality with Richter; as it were the central fire that pervades and vivifies his whole being. He is a humorist from his inmost soul; he thinks as a humorist, he feels, imagines, acts as a humorist: Sport is the element in which his nature lives and works. A tumultuous element for such a nature, and wild work he makes in it! A Titan in his sport as in his earnestness, he oversteps all bound, and riots without law or measure. He heaps Pelion upon Ossa, and hurls the universe together and asunder like a case of playthings. The Moon 'bombards' the Earth, being a rebellious satellite; Mars 'preaches' to the other planets, very singular doctrine; nay, we have Time and Space themselves playing fantastic tricks: it is an infinite masquerade; all Nature is gone forth mumming in the strangest guises.

Yet the anarchy is not without its purpose: these vizards are not mere hollow masks; there are living faces under them and this mumming has its significance. . . . Wayward as he seems, he works not without forethought: like Rubens, by a single stroke he can change a laughing face into a sad one. But in his smile itself a touching pathos may lie hidden, a pity too deep for tears. He is a man of feeling, in the noblest sense of that word; for he loves all living with the heart of a brother; his soul rushes forth, in sympathy with gladness and sorrow, with goodness or grandeur, over all Creation. . . .

That his manner of writing is singular, nay, in fact a wild complicated Arabesque, no one can deny. But the true question is, How nearly does this manner of writing represent his real manner of thinking and existing? . . . And why should we quarrel with the high, because it is not the highest? Richter's worst faults are nearly allied to his best merits; being chiefly exuberance of good, irregular squandering of wealth, a dazzling with excess of true light. These things may be pardoned the more readily, as they are little likely to be imitated. . . .

[Of] Richter's Philosophy . . . one only observation we shall make: it is not mechanical, or skeptical; it springs not from the forum or the laboratory, but from the depths of the human spirit; and yields as its fairest product a noble system of Morality, and the firmest conviction of Religion. . . . To a careless reader he might seem the wildest of infidels; for nothing can exceed the freedom with which he bandies to and fro the dogmas of religion, nay, sometimes, the highest objects of Christian reverence. . . . Yet, independently of all dogmas, nay, perhaps in spite of many, Richter is, in the highest sense of the word, religious. A reverence, not a self-interested fear, but a noble reverence for the spirit of all goodness, forms the crown and glory of his culture. . . . In this latter point we reckon him peculiarly worthy of study.[109]

Thus Carlyle's verdict on Jean Paul: valuable not only for revealing to us his powers of description but also for its relevance in our further consideration of his career. Even more remarkable was the article on the general "State of German Literature." It was a reply to the afore-mentioned anti-German tirades by the "elegant gentlemen" of George IV's era. The reproaches of mysticism and bad taste leveled against German culture could not have been refuted with more solid professional objectivity and confident eloquence than was done here. As a result of these articles Carlyle immediately took his place in the front rank of English authorities on German literature,[110] and in the light of the *Edinburgh Review*'s respected standing, it would be difficult to over-estimate his influence upon the advance of German studies in England. As an unmistakable sign of the growing interest in foreign culture, we mention only the *Foreign Review*, which began to appear a year later (1828) with Carlyle as a chief contributor. His excellent translations in *German Romance* met with all the more approval as he consulted English taste in the choice of works included and added biographical-critical essays on the lives and works of the German authors.

One further event of 1827* remains still to be mentioned: Carlyle's

* October 1826; ah me!

109. *Works*, XXVI, 14–15, 19, 20, 22.
110. The rest of the sentence is omitted in Althaus (1869) and replaced by "and his influence on the advancement of German studies in England dates especially from this time."

marriage with Miss Welsh, the daughter of Dr. Welsh, whose home he had visited frequently following his apprenticeship in Kirkcaldy.* His

* [*Carlyle crosses out the words "his apprenticeship in Kirkcaldy."*] [111]

marriage was childless, but happy otherwise. It was happy too in that his devoted, loving and congenial wife remained steadfast throughout his entire life and until her later years stood by his side, strong and erect as he was himself. Dr. Welsh presented the newly-weds with a property called Craigenputtoch in the north of Dumfriesshire, and soon after their marriage they went to live there.*

* This [*Carlyle refers to the entire paragraph*] is nearly all error together,—as is abundantly marked elsewhere. Dr Welsh had died, 1819, and never heard of me, much less saw me. Craigen-puttoch (not such a "*Gütchen*" [*property*], but really a *Landgut* [*estate*] in its kind, if you knew it) my beautiful Bride had, with my full consent (consent and *more*, had more, or so *much*, been requisite), given wholly over to her mother,—who had nothing else adequate to live upon; & who regularly received the rent of it (£200) from the Farmer beside us; nothing of it *ours*, but the big old Farm House (which we had, with many ingenious adjustments & contrivances, "repaired," at our own expence, into a very good & really handsome kind of Dwelling for us; building a *new* "Farm House," smaller, yet good enough that too), and one biggish Paddock for horses & cow;—there were we nestled, and had the comfort at all times of knowing that Farm or Mother suffered nothing by us. We were poor; in spite of my constancy at work, had perhaps hardly £100 of income, & that *not* regular, which was the sorest point of all; but (thanks to my incomparable little Jeannie!) we never wanted for any thing either of needful or even of really *elegant*, in the fine *simplex munditiis* [*simple neatness of*] [112] form appropriate to us;—and in my life, I have never elsewhere been so *well* lodged, fed, clad, kept and done-to, in all essential human respects; nor have seen (now that I look back

111. See note 38. Carlyle had resigned his teaching position in Kirkcaldy in November 1818.

112. Horace, Book I, Ode V ("Ad Pyrrham"), l. 5. Milton's translation is "plain in thy neatness."

on it, with *these* eyes) a poverty so noble! All *her* doing; thanks to her forever are due from me, who also strove to do my best.

Glimpses of our Life there are given in another Ms. To which I will add only: That the "Farmer beside us," for the first 3 or 2 years, was my next Brother, Alexander, an altogether ingenious, witty, shifty [*i.e.*, *resourceful*], valiant and indignant, yet tender & deeply affectionate man;[113] who contrived for us & self multifarious inventions and improvements in the original *chaos* there, till it became *cosmic* in fair measure: he was a great treasure to me, and something of a real companion too, having many thoughts in him, got from a certain modicum of good reading, and from much of serious reflexion, with a bright rustic faculty of insight, and fine just sympathies, to work by, in his limited world. He was given to banter, could be bitterly sarcastic, bitter and fiery on the dog-kind, for whom his contempt was infinite, his "tolerance" far too *small*. Yet I have heard from him touches of a most genial sense of the ridiculous, and little spurts of a mockery which was soft as new-milk just flavoured with the best *cognac*; and which tickled you into the very heart with a kindly laughter such as I might call superlative ["in my experience" *crossed out*]. How my poor Jeannie did enjoy these touches of his, & recited and repeated them in their wild Annandale accent!— My sister Mary (now at the Gill, a most kind-hearted, ingeniously frugal woman) kept house for Alick: the two, one or other of them, looked in on us often enough, affectionately respectful always; and as a rule dined with us every Sunday, where was usually good talk or reading.

This was really beautiful while it lasted; but, alas, it could not last forever. Misfortunes came, in this Alick Household; faults too there were, short-comings, misgoings; all of a smallish sort, and *in*voluntary all,—alas, none of us ever thought of considering them *voluntary*, or of regarding them as as [*sic*] other than "misfortunes" too, with pity for ourselves and them! Indeed, I

113. Alexander (Alick) Carlyle (1797–1876) farmed Craigenputtoch from 26 May 1827 to 26 May 1831. His sister Mary (1808–1888) kept house for him until her marriage late in 1830 to James Austin. Soon afterwards Alexander married Janet Clow (1809–1891).

have been told since, my poor Alick's grand *fault* was, he[114] had the Farm *too dear* (£200; & it is but £250 at the present high produce):—at any rate, he gave it up;[115] and Mrs Welsh's man of business let it to a Farmer of his own; with whom, as the fences were all tight, and the disposition peaceable on both sides, we had nothing farther to do. Very stupid people, farmer himself a kind of innocent zealously assiduous "two-leg[g]ed *Stot* [*ox*] in breeches," wife a pleasanter articulately speaking creature: both of whom, and all their caliban specimens, my Miranda tamed easily into perfect loyalty of admiration, and before long had them all at her charmed bidding, had that been necessary.— —[116] My Brother, after trial of various other enterprises, a bad new farm the first, found he was not prospering in his native country as infinitely stupider people were (he had wedded, too, before quitting Craigenputtoch, and was likely to have plenty of children), —got into disgust with his present position; & determined on emigrating. Did so (1843, I think);[117]—and is now an old man, with fine sons & daughters round him & partly well settled within reach, at "*Bield* near Brantford, Canada West"; not rich, but no longer embarras[s]ed; tilling his own acres, not another's; modestly prosperous, and looking over to us sad and quiet in his far-off little Kingdom & Patriarchate yonder. I love him much, and find something tragical & yet salutary and good in such a fate for a man of such gifts (some of them, *heroic* in their way) but also of such impatiences & indignations in an evil world. His eldest Son,

114. The younger Alexander Carlyle omits the passage from "Misfortunes came, in this Alick Household" through "he" in his typed transcript of Carlyle's notes to Althaus.

115. On 26 May 1831, because he could not meet the high rent. He lost £300 during the four years he worked the farm.

116. "Very stupid people" through "necessary" omitted in Alexander Carlyle's typed transcript. The "*Stot*" was Joseph M'Adam, "'some repeatedly-bankrupt Drover of these parts'" (TC to JAC, 4 March 1831, in Norton, *L26–36*, p. 195). In March 1831 he offered to lease the farm from Mrs. Welsh for £170 annually—£30 less than what Alexander had been paying. She accepted the offer.

117. After Alexander left Craigenputtoch he sought the mill at Annan and several other farms before finally renting Catlinns farm from 1832–1835. Still unsuccessful, he became a storekeeper in Annan in 1835, in Ecclefechan in 1838, and in 1843 emigrated to America. He stayed with his wife's relations in upper New York State in 1843–1844 and in 1844 bought the farm of Bield, Brantford-Paris, in Ontario, Canada.

"Tom," my namesake, seems to be a really fine fellow; and is now settled likewise, on a Farm of his own in those neighbourhoods; King (I trust, wisely) of One Man, if no other.[118] Craigenputtoch is now likely to go on lease to a son of my youngest Brother Jamie's;—*property* of it to be settled (if I can clearly see *how* with good effect) on Edinburgh University, as "John-Welsh Scholarships," or otherwise *well*, if so may be.[119] Enough now of Craigenputtoch,—once the "*Puttick* (or Small-Falcon) *Crag*," or Mountain, of whinstone, with Forest round it; where is now no *tree* but of man's planting.[120] *Her* Father was born there; the cradle, that, of his first 2 or 3 years in this world.

The year 1828 was even richer in literary works than the preceding year had been. Three articles came out in the *Foreign Review*—on Zacharias Werner, on Goethe's *Helena*, and on Goethe's *Collected Works*; and two in the *Edinburgh Review*—on Burns and on Johann Gottlob Heyne. Before discussing these articles, however, we should glance at Carlyle's newly established family life. The temptation to do so is all the greater in view of the very limited sources which afford a direct glimpse into his private affairs. A letter from Craigenputtoch, dated 25 September 1828, of Carlyle to Goethe, which Goethe includes in the preface to the German translation of the *Life of Schiller*, allows us a good opportunity. The picture sketched there is in itself so complete and characteristic that it scarcely requires an apology if we render verbatim the main body of the letter. "You inquire," Carlyle writes to Goethe,

118. Thomas Carlyle (1833–1921), eldest son of Alexander took in 1865 a farm on the Brantford-Paris highway that he called Bieldy Knowes. Another son, named for his father, is Alexander Carlyle (1843–1931), for whom see the capsule biography in Marrs, p. 552. The NLS holds a short unpublished autobiography (MS 739) "Jottings of Alexander Carlyle's Life and Work by Himself," written just before his death. It surveys his life and tells of his meetings with his famous uncle in the 1870's.

119. Carlyle did indeed leave Craigenputtoch in his will to the University of Edinburgh, the income to be used "for the foundation and endowment of ten equal bursaries to be called the 'John Welsh Bursaries'" (*Reminiscences*, I, 262). See pp. 261–277 for the complete deed of bequest. The University later disposed of the property, which is now owned by Mr. and Mrs. George Armour.

120. Cf. Froude, *Carlyle*, I, 108; and *Reminiscences*, I, 87–88: "'Craigen*puttock*,' or the stone-mountain, 'Craig' of the 'Puttock,'—puttock being a sort of *Hawk*, both in Galloway Speech, and in Shakespeare's Old English; 'Hill-Forest of the Puttocks,' now a very bare place, the universal silence was complete...." Norton notes the reference to *Cymbeline*, I, i, 139–140. After Carlyle settled at Craigenputtoch he usually spelled the name with an "h." That spelling has been followed in this edition.

with such affection touching our present abode and employments, that I must say some words on that subject, while I have still space. . . . Our dwelling-place is not in it [Dumfries]; but fifteen miles . . . to the Northwest of it, among the granite mountains and black moors, which stretch westward thro' Galloway almost to the Irish Sea. This is, as it were, a green oasis in that desart of heath and rock; a piece of ploughed and partially sheltered and ornamented ground where corn ripens, and trees yield umbrage, tho' encircled on all hands by moorfowl and only the hardiest breeds of sheep. Here, by dint of great endeavour, we have pargetted and garnished for ourselves a clean substantial dwelling; and settled down, in defect of any Professorial or other official appointment, to cultivate Literature on our own resources, by way of occupation; and roses and garden-shrubs, and if possible health, and a peaceable temper of mind, to forward it. The roses are indeed still mostly to plant; but they already blossom in Hope; and we have two swift horses, which, with the mountain air, are better than all physicians for sick nerves. That exercise, which I am very fond of, is almost my sole amusement; for this is one of the most solitary spots in Britain, being six miles from *any* individual of the formally visiting class. It might have suited Rousseau, almost as well as his Island of St. Pierre:[121] indeed I find that most of my city Friends impute to me a motive similar to his in coming hither, and predict no good from it. But I came hither purely for this one reason: That I might not have to write for bread; might not be tempted to tell lies for money. This space of Earth is our own; and we can live in it and write and think as seems best to us, tho' Zoilus[122] himself should become King of Letters. And as to its solitude, a Mail Coach will any day transport us to Edinburgh, which is our British Weimar[.] Nay even at this time, I have a whole horse-load of French, German, American, English Reviews and Journals, were they of any worth, encumbering the tables of my little Library. Moreover from any of our heights I can discern a Hill, a day's journey to the eastward, where Agricola with his Romans has left a camp,[123] at the foot of which I was born, where my Father and Mother are

121. An island in the middle of the Lake of Bienne, Switzerland, where Rousseau spent several idyllic months in the autumn of 1765.
122. A Greek of the fourth century B.C., who severely criticized Homer and Plato.
123. Birrens, or Blatum Bulgium, near Ecclefechan.

still living to love me. Time, therefore, must be left to try: but if I sink into folly, myself and not my situation will be to blame. Nevertheless I have many doubts about my future Literary activity; on all which how gladly would I take *your* counsel! Surely, you will write to me again, and ere long; that I may still feel myself united to you.[124]

Aside from frequent visits to Edinburgh and one trip to London, Carlyle lived in this philosophical, poetic solitude of Craigenputtoch until 1832 when he moved permanently to London.* Here he wrote most

* no; went up August *1831*, with *Sartor* in my pocket, intending to be back in a month; could not get *Sartor* published (Reform-Bill agitation &c &c); sent for my Wife, & passed the Winter there, making agreeable friends Leigh Hunt, John Mill, &c and experiences;—returned (still with *Sartor* in my pocket), March 1832. Had lost my good, my strong & great old Father in the interim; my *Goethe* shortly after my return: we were in a high & serious, not a miserable or pining frame of mind. I wrote *Diamond Necklace, Cagliostro*, and various things (*translation* a good part of them, *Mährchen* &c);[125] was publishing *Sartor*, slit in Pieces (but rigorously *un*altered otherwise) in *Fraser's Magazine*; had a visit from Edward Irving (pleasant 30 hours, one of those Summers);[126] —at length, in May 1834 actually 'übersiedelte' [*moved*], to the House where I still am; I alone left.—

of the essays which have advanced the recognition of German culture in England more than those of any other international figure. Here he resolved to devote in a certain sense* this period of his life to this work in

* in *all* senses!

order that he might bring to the fore, in a new field and in new subjects, the wealth of his knowledge and the deeply-rooted strength of his convictions. The restrictions of the space made available to us do not permit our dwelling on these superb essays in as much detail as their rich content

124. Text: *CL*, IV, 407–408.
125. Upon returning to Craigenputtoch Carlyle translated Goethe's "The Tale" and "Novelle"; the "Death of Goethe," "Goethe's Works," and "Diderot" were among the "various things" he wrote at this time.
126. Actually 8–9 June 1829. See *Reminiscences*, II, 186–189.

merits. We can only recommend them generally as true models of literary criticism of our countrymen and call attention to individual points, the consideration of which is of especial interest in viewing Carlyle's character.

Above all, to the foregoing statements from his correspondence with Goethe, we should add several others which express his enthusiasm for Goethe as man and poet. For however decisively Jean Paul, Fichte and other well-known figures in German culture influenced Carlyle's development, he still looked up to no one with deeper or more lasting reverence than he did to Goethe. He was convinced that Goethe was the greatest man of the last two centuries.[127] How his deep and lasting regard for Goethe affected his entire thinking was shown recently in his inaugural address as Rector of the University of Edinburgh. There, in reviewing the experiences of a very long life, he declared, as he looked into the future of the young people to whom he spoke, that if ambition had been his only rule he would rather have written or been able to write the tenth and eleventh chapters of *Wilhelm Meister's Travels*, pages full of a mature priestly wisdom which in his opinion nothing since* written has

* **oder lange vordem** [*or long before*](!)

equalled.[128] For this reason, after the translation of *Wilhelm Meister*, he reverted again and again to consideration of the genius of Goethe. Few of his writings fail to refer to the old master of the art of life whom he revered as the greatest intellectual hero of our time. We have already mentioned his two articles of 1828 on Goethe and wish here to call immediate attention to the four others on him which followed in 1832 in the *Edinburgh Review** and in *Fraser's Magazine*. It is difficult to choose

* ? no.[129]

from such an abundance of material; for our purposes the following passage will have to suffice. "In Goethe's mind," Carlyle wrote,

127. Carlyle frequently expressed this conviction, e.g., *Works*, V, 158.

128. For Carlyle's translation of these pages in *Wilhelm Meister*, see *Works*, XXIV, 258–278. My translation, as does Althaus's German paraphrase, closely echoes the wording of Carlyle's inaugural address in *Works*, XXIX, 473.

129. None of the essays on Goethe or translations of his works which Carlyle did in 1832 appeared in the *Edinburgh Review*, whose pages, with Macvey Napier replacing Jeffrey as editor, had gradually become closed to him. "Goethe's Portrait" appeared in *Fraser's Magazine*, 5 (March 1832), 206. Goethe died on 22 March 1832.

the first aspect that strikes us is its calmness, then its beauty; a deeper inspection reveals to us its vastness and unmeasured strength. This man rules, and is not ruled. The stern and fiery energies of a most passionate soul lie silent in the centre of his being; a trembling sensibility has been inured to stand, without flinching or murmur, the sharpest trials. Nothing outward, nothing inward, shall agitate or control him. The brightest and most capricious fancy, the most piercing and inquisitive intellect, the wildest and deepest imagination; the highest thrills of joy, the bitterest pangs of sorrow: all these are his, he is not theirs. . . . He is king of himself and of his world; nor does he rule it like a vulgar great man, like a Napoleon or Charles Twelfth, by the mere brute exertion of his will, grounded on no principle, or on a false one: his faculties and feelings are not fettered or prostrated under the iron sway of Passion, but led and guided in kindly union under the mild sway of Reason; as the fierce primeval elements of Nature were stilled at the coming of Light, and bound together, under its soft vesture, into a glorious and beneficent Creation.

This is the true Rest of man. . . ; the dim aim of every human soul, the full attainment of only a chosen few. It comes not unsought to any; but the wise are wise because they think no price too high for it. Goethe's inward home has been reared by slow and laborious efforts; but it stands on no hollow or deceitful basis: for his peace is not from blindness, but from clear vision; not from uncertain hope of alteration, but from sure insight into what cannot alter. His world seems once to have been desolate and baleful as that of the darkest sceptic: but he has covered it anew with beauty and solemnity, derived from deeper sources, over which Doubt can have no sway. He has inquired fearlessly, and fearlessly searched out and denied the False; but he has not forgotten, what is equally essential and infinitely harder, to search out and admit the True. His heart is still full of warmth, though his head is clear and cold; the world for him is still full of grandeur, though he clothes it with no false colours; his fellow-creatures are still objects of reverence and love, though their basenesses are plainer to no eye than to his. To reconcile these contradictions is the task of all good men, each for himself, in his own way and manner; a task which, in our age, is encompassed with

71

difficulties peculiar to the time; and which Goethe seems to have accomplished with a success that few can rival.[130]

In these words we have the credo of a man who has as his calling to express "the Divine Idea of the World,"[131] not merely to deny the false but equally to affirm the true, expressed in a new form. We also see the idea of hero-worship (a subject of immense significance in Carlyle's later thought) foreshadowed in the admiration for the success of a great man in the fulfillment of that calling. Carlyle had by now grown accustomed to view the existence of mankind and of individual humans from this point of view and to measure according to this ideal standard the worth of individual actions and of historical events. The period of doubt sank*

* *had* quite sunk, and got done with sinking, above 7 years before.[132]

behind him into the past. Belief in the true, the good, and the beautiful, with full consciousness of his responsibility in the struggle to realize this belief—the struggle to preserve the universe against chaos in all things—had become his religion, and with religious seriousness and fervor he set out to accomplish the work which this belief imposed upon him. For years he had striven for light and truth with only impassioned longing and in bitter suffering, and, under the guidance of the great poets and philosophers, he had sought to find the eternal guiding stars on the right path.[133] But a mind with such depth and fierce energy as his could never rest with these achievements. The time came when he had to step forth from the world of the imagination into the world of reality. He lived in a period of transition that was skeptical and anarchical, more analytical than creative, more materialistic than idealistic, a period in which the old beliefs of mankind were casualties of the age and which only occasionally recognized the scattered elements needed for the construction of a new one. This circumstance and the fact of his own manly courage, his fearless love of truth and his brilliant literary talent— in which the imagination of a poet and prophet fuses with the intellectual

130. *Works*, XXIII, 23–25. This passage, from the preface to *Wilhelm Meister's Apprenticeship* (1824), Carlyle published virtually unchanged in his 1828 essay "Goethe" (*Works*, XXVI, 246–247).

131. See note 59.

132. During his year of tranquillity at Hoddam Hill in 1825–1826. See notes 64, 89, 101.

133. This sentence is omitted in Althaus (1869).

boldness of a great thinker[134]—offer the most profound basis of explanation for his later works and for the phenomenon, unique in its way, of his subsequent activity.

In the meantime, before we pass to the second phase in the development of Carlyle's career, we have still to glance briefly at the last memorials, written during the Craigenputtoch years, of his unwearied diligence with German literature.* Aside from the studies on Heyne and Goethe, these

* all written at Craigenputtoch.

included articles on recent German dramatists and on Novalis (1829), a second essay on Jean Paul (1830), and, lastly, shorter or longer discussions of Luther, Schiller, the *Nibelungenlied*, and German literature of the fourteenth and fifteenth centuries. Several of these articles appeared in the *Foreign Review* and in *Fraser's Magazine*, others in the *Edinburgh Review*, and one in the recently*-founded *Westminster Review*. Moreover,

* [*Carlyle crosses out "recently" and substitutes*] alt [*old, i.e., long-established.*] [*He adds:*] (if you mean the *Nibelungen*!)[135]

these were not the only works of those years. The essay on Burns mentioned earlier also provides a fine example of Carlyle's wide knowledge of English literary history, and a long essay on Voltaire, written in 1829, reveals how thoroughly he knew eighteenth-century French literature. He wrote in the same year the first draft of the often-cited *Sartor Resartus*, a cosmic-biographical, allegorical-symbolical work composed in Jean Paul's style and modelled after him. In this work, Carlyle summed up the history of his own inward and outward struggles and the outcome of his life's philosophy. With the manuscript of this remarkable book in hand, he went to London for the second time in 1830* to look for a publisher.

* [*Carlyle crosses out the "o" and writes*] '31 (I rather think).[136]

But no publisher was to be found. The booksellers' advisors, or "booksellers' tasters," as he humorously called them,[137] declared that, although

---

134. "In which . . . thinker" omitted in Althaus (1869).

135. The *Westminster Review*, founded in 1824 by James Mill, was amalgamated with the *London Review* in 1836 and emerged as the *London and Westminster Review*. Carlyle published "The Nibelungen Lied" in 15 (July 1831), 1–45.

136. August 1831.

137. In the appendix "Testimonies of Authors," which first appeared in the 1838 English edition (reprinted in Harrold, *Sartor*, pp. 319–320), and in "Characteristics" (1831), *Works*, XXVIII, 24–25.

there was no denying the intelligence and talent of the author, the work was too eccentric and whimsical to suit the public's "taste." His purpose unaccomplished, Carlyle returned with his manuscript from the turmoil of London to the solitude of Craigenputtoch. Further attempts* to

* there were none made.

publish *Sartor Resartus* as a book also proved unsuccessful, so that it only came out, apparently much revised,* in 1833–1834 in *Fraser's*

* Not a letter of it altered; except in the *last* and the *first* page, a word or two!— — Nothing whatever of "*spätere Versuche*" [*further attempts*] either (as already marked):[138] Fraser's Public liked the *Johnson* so much (which I had left with him, written there that winter)[139] that he was willing to accept *Sartor* in the slit condition; had it so (probably on cheaper terms),[140] went on with it obstinately till done,—tho', from his Public, he had a sore time with it: "What wretched unintelligible nonsense!" "Sir, if you publish any more of that d——d [*stuff?*], I shall be obliged to give up my Magazine!" and so forth,[141] —in the whole world (so far as could be learned) only two persons dissentient, 1° a certain man called *Emerson*, in Concord Massachusetts,[142] and 2° a certain

138. Carlyle makes here the important disclosure that he did not alter significantly the manuscript of *Sartor* (completed late in July 1831) between its several rejections by London publishers in the autumn of 1831 and its serial publication in *Fraser's Magazine* (November and December 1833, February-April, June-August 1834). Contrary to general opinion (e.g., Harrold, *Sartor*, p. xxvi, based on Wilson, *Carlyle*, II, 322), he did not submit it to Edinburgh publishers after the attempts in London had failed. Elsewhere in the notes to Althaus Carlyle stresses that, in changing nothing in *Sartor* except on the first and last pages, he bent neither to public opinion nor to pressure from the magazine's publisher, James Fraser. That he made no significant alterations in *Sartor* became a point of honor with him. G. B. Tennyson correctly notes, however, that in February 1833 Carlyle emended the name "Teufelsdreck" to the more subtle "Teufelsdröckh" (*Sartor*, p. 152).

139. Of 1831–1832, which the Carlyles spent in London. "Boswell's Life of Johnson" was published in *Fraser's Magazine*, 5 (May 1832), 379–413.

140. Carlyle hoped to earn £200 from the serialization of *Sartor* in *Fraser's*, but received only £82/1/0 and 58 copies stitched together from the magazine's sheets.

141. Cf. Moncure D. Conway, *Thomas Carlyle* (New York: Harper, 1881), pp. 71–72. Carlyle in his correspondence of 1834 took wry pleasure in speaking of the "unqualified disapproval" which *Sartor* met.

142. Emerson had written Fraser during the 1833–1834 winter: "Send me *Fraser* so long as 'Sartor' continues in it" (p. 72 of Conway, *Carlyle*, cited in previous note). Although Joseph Slater pointed out that "since this sentence is Conway's version of

Irish Catholic Priest, Father O'Shea of Cork (whom I have seen since, & who yet lives) writing to him, each for himself, "So long as any thing by that man appears in your Magazine, punctually send it me."[143] So that Fraser conceived a certain terror, if also a certain respect, of my writings & me; and knew not what to do,—beyond standing by his bargain, with an effort. Poor Soul, he was in the hands of a set of Maginns, Father Prouts, J. A. Herauds &c &c, partly of the clever Irish-Blackguard type, partly of the pure English Vapid-Blockhead ditto;[144] and was not a man of adventurous temper, or of deep judgement. In a year or two after *French Revolution* (for which I never received the colour of coin from him),[145] he died;—and I remember reading, in some Newspaper Obituary, what a "generous patron he had been to Thomas Carlyle,"—thank you for nothing or for less!——[146]

Magazine, and not until 1837 was it published in London as a book in its own right (after an American edition had appeared in Boston the year

---

Carlyle's recollection, thirty years later, of Fraser's oral quotation from Emerson's letter, it may not be verbatim" (*CEC*, p. 16), Carlyle's more vigorous language in the note to Althaus confirms that Conway correctly caught the gist of his statement. In May 1834, writing his first letter to Carlyle, Emerson mentioned that he had "now received four numbers of the Sartor Resartus for whose light, thanks evermore" (Slater, *CEC*, p. 98).

143. Cf. Carlyle's journal entry of 26 July 1834, in Froude, *Carlyle*, I, 445, and Slater, *CEC*, p. 103. Carlyle eventually met Father O'Shea in Cork and described his encounter in *Reminiscences of My Irish Journey in 1849* (London: Sampson Low, 1882), pp. 116–117.

144. William Maginn (1793–1842), born in Cork; F. S. Mahony (1804–1866), also born in Cork and best known under the pseudonym of "Father Prout"; John Abraham Heraud (1799–1887), born in London. Maginn and "Father Prout" qualify by their Irish birth to be "of the clever Irish-Blackguard type," Heraud by his English birth to be "of the pure English Vapid-Blockhead ditto." See Miriam M. H. Thrall, *Rebellious Fraser's: Nol Yorke's Magazine in the Days of Maginn, Thackeray, and Carlyle* (New York: Columbia University Press, 1934).

145. Emerson however remitted Carlyle £150 in all from the sale of the first American edition.

146. James Fraser (d. 2 Oct. 1841), owner and publisher of *Fraser's Magazine* was Carlyle's publisher through *Heroes and Hero-Worship* (1841). Carlyle probably alludes to the obituary in *Fraser's Magazine*, 24 (Nov. 1841), 626–628. It reprinted a notice from the *Inverness Courier*, which said in part: "To one distinguished literary man of the day—Thomas Carlyle—Mr. Fraser was a kind and generous friend" (p. 628).

before).[147] In considering Carlyle's intellectual development, it is essential to understand the times in which *Sartor Resartus* was written, and we have thus spared no effort to ascertain the right date. This was easier to do with respect to the two articles in the *Edinburgh Review*,[148] which are hardly less important and in fact are comparable to *Sartor* in that they may be considered landmarks in the transition from one stage of his life to another[149] and in that they move out of the sphere of literature into the wide field of time. One of these dates from that productive year of his life, 1829, and bears the significant title "Signs of the Times." The other came out in 1831 and under the laconic title "Characteristics"* comprises

* The last thing I had written at Craigenputtoch before setting off for London in 1831.[150]

one of the most profound and stylistically most perfect philosophical expressions of Carlyle's thought. Both essays arise, apparently, from the same basic way of thinking, and with *Sartor Resartus* cast a revealing light on the times in which they were written and on the year which followed. Let us therefore recall that Carlyle, though still residing at Craigenputtoch, was about to move to London, and, before accompanying him there, let us attempt to find in these two essays a reflection of his attitude toward the state of the contemporary world and of the prevailing mood at the time when he took up residence in that mighty center of modern life.

This attitude was predominantly a serious, gloomy, and melancholy one. "Were we required to characterise this age of ours by any single epithet," he observes in "Signs of the Times,"

we should be tempted to call it, not an Heroical, Devotional, Philosophical, or Moral Age, but, above all others, the Mechanical Age. It is the Age of Machinery, in every outward and inward sense of that word; the age which, with its whole undivided might, forwards, teaches and practises the great art of adapting means to ends. Nothing

147. The first English edition appeared in 1838, not 1837.
148. "Signs of the Times," 49 (June 1829), 439–459; "Characteristics," 54 (Dec. 1831), 351–383.
149. Changed in Althaus (1869) to "from the earlier stage of his life to the new stage which now follows."
150. Carlyle errs in his dating of "Characteristics": he wrote it *after* he arrived in London.

is now done directly, or by hand; all is by rule and calculated contrivance....[151]

We have machines for Education.... We have Religious machines. ... Philosophy, Science, Art, Literature, all depend on machinery. ... Has any man, or any society of men, a truth to speak, a piece of spiritual work to do; they can nowise proceed at once and with the mere natural organs, but must first call a public meeting, appoint committees, issue prospectuses, eat a public dinner; in a word, construct or borrow machinery, wherewith to speak it and do it.... No Newton, by silent meditation, now discovers the system of the world from the falling of an apple; but some quite other than Newton stands in his Museum, his Scientific Institution, and behind whole batteries of retorts, digesters, and galvanic piles imperatively "interrogates Nature." ... In defect of Raphaels, and Angelos, and Mozarts, we have Royal Academies of Painting, Sculpture, Music. ... Literature, too, has its Paternoster-row mechanism, its Trade-dinners, its Editorial conclaves, and huge subterranean, puffing bellows; so that books are not only printed, but, in a great measure, written and sold, by machinery.[152]

No Queen Christina, in these times, needs to send for her Descartes; no King Frederick for his Voltaire.... Any sovereign of taste, who wishes to enlighten his people, has only to impose a new tax, and with the proceeds establish Philosophic Institutes.... In like manner, among ourselves, when it is thought that religion is declining, we have only to vote half-a-million's worth of bricks and mortar, and build new churches.[153]

Nay.... the whole discontent of Europe takes this [mechanical][154] direction. The deep, strong cry of all civilised nations,—a cry which, everyone now sees, must and will be answered, is: Give us a reform of Government! A good structure of legislation, a proper check upon the executive, a wise arrangement of the judiciary, is *all* that is wanting for human happiness. The Philosopher of this age is not a Socrates, a

151. *Works*, XXVII, 59. I have begun a new paragraph whenever Carlyle indicates one.
152. *Works*, XXVII, 61–62. Althaus reverses the order of the sentences beginning "Has any man" and "No Newton"; I retain his order. He adds in a note that "Paternoster Row is the street in London for booksellers *par excellence*."
153. Ibid., p. 62.
154. My insertion.

Plato, . . . who inculcates on men the necessity and infinite worth of moral goodness, the great truth that our happiness depends on the mind which is within us, and not on the circumstances which are without us; but a Smith, a De Lolme, a Bentham, who chiefly inculcates the reverse of this,—that our happiness depends entirely on external circumstances; nay, that the strength and dignity of the mind within us is itself the creature and consequence of these. . . . Thus is the Body-politic more than ever worshipped and tendered; but the Soul-politic less than ever. Love of country, in any high or generous sense, in any other than an almost animal sense, or mere habit, has little importance attached to it in such reforms, or in the opposition shown them. Men are to be guided only by their self-interests.[155]

*Indeed, we need only recall that this wholly mechanical behavior and

* n. l [*new line, i.e., new paragraph*].

its consequences are not the ultimate objects; that the mechanical principle is inferior to the dynamic; and that the most perfect material thing creates no happiness if it lacks the life-giving spirit. Not in this way did great men and historical events have their impact. Though they did not ignore the mechanical, in each case their innermost being was of a dynamic character; above all, it leads to the endeavor to order, to purify, and to strengthen man's intrinsic natural powers.

The Reformation had an invisible, mystic and ideal aim; the result was indeed to be embodied in external things; but its spirit, its worth was internal, invisible, infinite. Our English Revolution too originated in Religion. Men did battle, in those old days, not for Purse-sake, but for Conscience-sake. Nay, in our own days, it is no way different. The French Revolution itself had something higher in it than cheap bread and a Habeas-corpus act. Here too was an Idea; a Dynamic, not a Mechanic force. It was a struggle, though a blind and at last an insane one, for the infinite, divine nature of Right, of Freedom, of Country.

Thus does man, in every age, vindicate, consciously or unconsciously, his celestial birthright. Thus does Nature hold on her wondrous, unquestionable course; and all our systems and theories are but so many froth-eddies or sand-banks, which from time to

155. *Works*, XXVII, 66–67.

time she casts up, and washes away. When we can drain the Ocean into mill-ponds, and bottle-up the Force of Gravity, to be sold by retail, in gas jars; then may we hope to comprehend the infinitudes of man's soul under formulas of Profit and Loss; and rule over this too, as over a patent engine, by checks, and valves, and balances.[156]

A similar train of thought is evident in "Characteristics." The essay begins with the ancient Hippocratic maxim: "The healthy know not of their health, but only the sick."[157] It contrasts, on the one hand, the less sophisticated times which unconsciously created from the depths of the spirit those men of genius whose highest revelations arise freely and untrammeled as from the chaos, with, on the other hand, our self-conscious, self-admiring age and society which ponders the future, seeks to know the reasons for things, and still despairs—and whose characteristic condition thus appears to the serious thinker not as health, but as disease. "Well," he exclaims (and we encounter here for the first time one of Carlyle's favorite ideas, one he never wearied of repeating throughout his life with the pathos of deep conviction),

> Well might the Ancients make Silence a god; for it is the element of all godhood, infinitude, or transcendental greatness; at once the source and the ocean wherein all such begins and ends. In the same sense, too, have Poets sung "Hymns to the Night"; as if Night were nobler than Day; as if Day were but a small motley-coloured veil spread transiently over the infinite bosom of Night, and did but deform and hide us its purely transparent eternal deeps. So likewise have they spoken and sung as if Silence were the grand epitome and complete sum-total of all Harmony; and Death, what mortals call Death, properly the beginning of Life.[158]

If on the other hand we examine the state of society in our time, we find that it "is, of all possible states, the least an unconscious one. . . ."

> What, for example, is all this that we hear, for the last generation or two, about the Improvement of the Age, the Spirit of the Age, Destruction of Prejudice, Progress of the Species, and the March of Intellect, but an unhealthy state of self-sentience, self-survey; the

156. *Works*, XXVII, 71.
157. Ibid., XXVIII, 1.
158. Ibid., pp. 16–17. The poet of *Hymns to the Night* is Friedrich von Hardenberg (1772–1801), or "Novalis."

precursor and prognostic of still worse health? That Intellect do march, if possible at double-quick time, is very desirable; nevertheless, why should she turn round at every stride, and cry: See you what a stride I have taken!* Such a marching of Intellect is distinctly of

* !

the spavined kind. . . .[159]

Till at length indeed, we have come to such a pass, that except in this same *medicine* [which we recognize as symptoms of the disease], with its artifices and appliances, few can so much as imagine any strength or hope to remain for us. The whole Life of Society must now be carried on by drugs: doctor after doctor appears with his nostrum, of Coöperative Societies, Universal Suffrage, Cottage-and-Cow systems, Repression of Population, Vote by Ballot. . . .[160]

Still the disease will not be healed: it is not merely a spiritual but also a physical disease.

Wealth has accumulated itself into masses; and Poverty, also in accumulation enough, lies impassably separated from it; opposed, uncommunicating, like forces in positive and negative poles. The gods of this lower world sit aloft on glittering thrones, less happy than Epicurus's gods, but as indolent, as impotent; while the boundless living chaos of Ignorance and Hunger welters terrific, in its dark fury, under their feet. . . . [Man] has subdued this Planet, his habitation and inheritance; yet reaps no profit from the victory. . . . Countries are rich, prosperous in all manner of increase, beyond example: but the Men of those countries are poor, needier than ever of all sustenance outward and inward; of Belief, of Knowledge, of Money, of Food. . . . Sad to look upon: in the highest stage of civilisation, nine tenths of mankind have to struggle in the lowest battle of savage or even animal man, the battle against Famine.[161]

If misery was the lot of other times, still they at least had a faith which supported them.

Now this is specially the misery which has fallen on man in our Era. Belief, Faith has well-nigh vanished from the world. The youth

159. *Works*, XXVIII, 18.
160. Ibid., pp. 19–20. Althaus inserts the clause in brackets.
161. Ibid., pp. 20–21. Althaus reverses the order of the last two sentences.

on awakening in this wondrous Universe no longer finds a competent theory of its wonders. . . . Mother Church has, to the most, become a superannuated Step-mother, whose lessons go disregarded; or are spurned at, and scornfully gainsaid. . . . The old ideal of Manhood has grown obsolete, and the new is still invisible to us, and we grope after it in darkness, one clutching this phantom, another that; Werterism, Byronism, even Brummelism, each has its day. . . . The Thinker must, in all senses, wander homeless, too often aimless, looking up to a Heaven which is dead for him, round to an Earth which is deaf. . . .[162]

A sad fate indeed! Sad in the highest degree because we know nothing more than that this endless change is universal and unavoidable.

*Still, the gloomy picture has its other side.

* n. 1 [*new line*].

Nay, if we look well to it, what is all Derangement, and necessity of great Change, in itself such an evil, but the product simply of *increased resources* which the old *methods* can no longer administer; of new wealth which the old coffers will no longer contain? What is it, for example, that in our own day bursts asunder the bonds of ancient Political Systems, and perplexes all Europe with the fear of Change, but even this: the increase of social resources, which the old social methods will no longer sufficiently administer? The new omnipotence of the Steam-engine is hewing asunder quite other mountains than the physical. . . . It is true again, the ancient methods of administration will no longer suffice. Must the indomitable millions, full of old Saxon energy and fire, lie cooped-up in this Western Nook, choking one another, as in the Blackhole of Calcutta, while a whole fertile untenanted Earth, desolate for want of the ploughshare, cries: Come and till me, come and reap me? If the ancient Captains can no longer yield guidance, new must be sought after: for the difficulty lies not in nature, but in artifice; the European Calcutta-Blackhole has no walls but air ones and paper ones.— — So too, Scepticism itself, with its innumerable mischiefs, what is it but the sour fruit of a most blessed increase, that of Knowledge; a fruit too that will not always continue *sour*? . . .

162. Ibid., pp. 29–30.

The fever of Scepticism must needs burn itself out, and burn out thereby the Impurities that caused it; then again will there be clearness, health. The principle of life, which now struggles painfully, in the outer, thin and barren domain of the Conscious or Mechanical, may then withdraw into its inner sanctuaries, its abysses of mystery and miracle; withdraw deeper than ever into that domain of the Unconscious, by nature infinite and inexhaustible; and creatively work there. From that mystic region, and from that alone, all wonders, all Poesies, and Religions and Social Systems have proceeded: the like wonders, and greater and higher, lie slumbering there; and, brooded on by the spirit of the waters, will evolve themselves, and rise like exhalations from the Deep.[163]

These excerpts not only throw a clear light on Carlyle's state of mind and philosophical position at the time but also contain in essence the distinctive features of his social philosophy. However often he later returned to this subject and however varied the phenomena in contemporary political and social life[164] to which he directed his attention, his train of thought and his philosophical conclusions always remained fundamentally the same. In ringing tones, there resounds again and again the elegaic and prophetic lament over the decline of the former age of faith, the profound and melancholy recognition of the shortcomings and sufferings of our age, the plea for idealism rather than materialism, for the deed rather than the word, for the resolute life in the true, the good, and the beautiful rather than the easy life in superficialities, self-deceptions, and half-truths. Again and again his hand has pointed through the present deafening noise of battle to the rebirth of the better future that the very sickness of the present presages. He felt he was too much a citizen of his own age—a soldier in the great human struggle—to be able to rest with his philosophy in a haven of peace. However, if all discords and the whole chaotic and revolutionary conflict of our age emerge explosively in his works, and it often appears that his philosophy will end in a wild cry of despair, yet beneath these stormy waves the foundations of his convictions still stand on firm ground and the ultimate result of his thinking is the challenge to serve truth in one's life, work and aspirations. This battle-cry

163. Ibid., pp. 39–40.
164. "Contemporary political and social life" changed in Althaus (1869) to "public life."

can never be repeated often enough. Carlyle repeated it recently to his audience in Edinburgh,[165] and anyone wishing to understand him should always bear in mind this synthesis not only of all his dissonances but also of his work and of his hope.

In *Sartor Resartus*, the last work written at Craigenputtoch, which, as noted already, Carlyle brought back with him as a manuscript in 1832*

*[*Carlyle crosses out "2" and substitutes*] 1.

from London and, in many respects* revised, and which came out during

* ganz und gar nicht [*not at all*].[166]

1833–1834 in *Fraser's Magazine*, we first encounter another of his characteristic traits: the first signs of his sense of humor. At the same time it is that work of Carlyle's[167] which may be viewed as marking the transition between two periods of his life: it is both a memorial to past struggles and a guide to his future life and work. Limitations of space preclude our entering into detail concerning its composition and basic argument.[168] We mention only, to explain the strange title, that the ostensible subject is a "philosophy of clothes" and that the author developed it from an alleged work of the German scholar Diogenes Teufelsdröckh, Professor of Things-in-General at the University of Weissnichtwo, a work which was recently published in the above-named university town by the firm of Stillschweigen & Co. under the title *Clothes, their Origin and Influence*.[169] The editor, an old friend of Teufelsdröckh's, undertook to acquaint the English public with the essentials of the philosophy of clothes and in the course of doing this promised a biography of Teufelsdröckh, for which a mutual acquaintance, Privy Counsellor Heuschrecke, had supplied him with the source materials. The excerpts quoted earlier—which undoubtedly hint at Carlyle's own development—are taken from this biographical part of *Sartor*. As far as the philosophy of clothes is concerned, it gives an

165. At his inaugural address as Rector of the University of Edinburgh, delivered 2 April 1866.

166. See note 138. Carlyle brought the manuscript of *Sartor* back with him to Craigenputtoch in 1832, not 1831.

167. Changed in Althaus (1869) to "It is a masterpiece of that time."

168. The sentence is omitted in Althaus (1869).

169. Carlyle's translation of the German title. Harrold, *Sartor*, p. 8, gives English equivalents of the German names.

imaginative, half-profound (in the Faustian sense), half-humorous development (following Jean Paul) of the teachings of transcendental idealism: that the whole world of appearances is really only a symbol, a temporal veil over the eternal ideas which "at the roaring Loom of Time"[170] weave *"the living visible Garment of God."*[171] The contrast between this idealism and the actual condition of things in the state, in the church, and in society, the application of the philosophy of clothes to human history, from Eden and fig-leaves right up to the latest manifestation in the sect of our modern dandies, opens a limitless field to humor. This serious depth of concern for the transcendental and the ideal on the one hand, and its rough confrontation with the humdrum on the other, characterizes Carlyle's humor in general. We hear from him neither the flippant laugh of the sceptic nor the outbreak of unrestrained mirth in which the humorous novelist and writer disengages himself from the oppressive burden of reflection. In its effect his humor often recalls Rembrandt. His comic chiaroscuro arises from the shining of the light of the eternal ideas—of the glare of the flames of the decline and rebirth of the world—into the seething chaos of final shapes and forms which emerge from the abyss, wander through the ages over the earth, and again sink down into the abyss. Thus we see mankind and individual human beings in a splendid light as the fusion of two infinities, the great and the small, the selfish and the domineering, ruling and being ruled, at sport and at war. We see man's attempts, desperate and only partly effective, to move from the darkness and the twilight to the full sunshine of life. The author, as guide, explains to us the course of this drama. He is moved by turns to laughter and tears, to pity and grief, to disgust and scorn, to satirical bitterness and fiery inspiration. However, he soon returns from all his changing moods to that most basic ground-tone, and the ringing laughter, in which he at times forgot himself, dies away in the mournful chords of a nocturne. Similarly, his hero Teufelsdröckh—after he has rushed violently through the whole world of philosophy and history and (like a new Peter Schlemihl[172]) through the entire inhabited earth from the Atlantic to the Pacific Ocean and from the North to the

---

170. See the Earth Spirit's speech in *Faust* I, l. 508 (Harrold, *Sartor*, p. 55).

171. Carlyle's phrase in Harrold, *Sartor*, p. 55, paraphrasing *Faust* I, l. 509.

172. The title character of Adelbert von Chamisso's allegorical tale (1814), who sells his shadow to the devil in return for the purse of Fortunatus and equipped with seven-league boots crisscrosses the earth.

South Pole—finds peace at last in the *"Divine Depth of Sorrow."*[173] Here he is summoned to work as long as day lasts, in the conditions in which he finds himself and in the moment in time in which he lives, and to realize as best he can the divine idea of the world before "the night cometh, when no man can work."[174] As to mankind at present, his "philosophy of clothes" taught him that man has dragged himself slowly about in the obsolete garments of the church, of the state, and of society— obsolete because the life-creating spirit had disappeared and because the forms were no longer one with the ideas. Still, Carlyle conceives man in the image of a self-immolating phoenix, from whose ashes a rejuvenated mankind will arise in more majestic form.[175]

In this mood and with these ideas in his mind and heart, Carlyle moved in 1832* from Craigenputtoch to London. Goethe died in this year and,

*[*Carlyle crosses out "2" and substitutes*] 4.

curiously enough, it was also the year in which Carlyle ceased his long study of German literature. His studies had borne fruit. Already three years before he had been able to write to Goethe "that a knowledge and appreciation of Foreign, especially of German literature is spreading with increased rapidity over all the domain of the English Tongue . . . that even in Oxford and Cambridge . . . which have all along been regarded as the strongholds of Insular pride and prejudice, there is a strange stir in this matter."[176] In 1830 the German translation of his *Life of Schiller* had appeared with the preface by Goethe from which we have so often quoted. With a sure consciousness of having done his share in this international exchange of ideas, he could now turn to a new sphere of intellectual activity. In the course of the year 1832* the *Monthly*

* Summer time 1832; I remember it well. Written on Lytton Bulwer's request, who was then Editor of that extinct *Magazine*.

Magazine published his obituary notice of Goethe, the *Foreign Review*

173. Harrold, *Sartor*, pp. 189, 193.
174. John 9:14, and cf. Eccles. 9:10. See also the ending of "The Everlasting Yea": "Work while it is called Today; for the Night cometh, wherein no man can work" (Harrold, *Sartor*, p. 197).
175. "The Phoenix," chap. V of Book III in *Sartor*.
176. Carlyle to Goethe, 22 December 1829, in Norton, *GC*, p. 162 (corrected against manuscript).

his long study of Goethe's works,[177] *Fraser's Magazine* his comments on Goethe's and Schiller's relationship with Madame de Staël and translations of Goethe's "Märchen" and "Novelle." After this he turned his back upon German literature and began instead to study French literature and history of the eighteenth century.* The purpose of these studies was

* had from of old been at that; by no means then 'began' that!

not so much the ideas themselves in French literature as it was their relationship to the occurrence which he saw as the greatest historical event of recent times: the French Revolution. Tired of the old world and of its endless confusion, he had already thought* a number of times of

* There is a kind of truth in this; I really had such a thought occasionally in my head, while toiling over the *French Revolution* Book on those grim terms: but the chief ground of it was, All honest, not *dis*honest, means of *livelihood* (Book-writing included, for who, *teste* [*according to*] Fraser &c, could be expected to buy such a Book?) seemed to be shut against me in the old world. "Very well," thought I (amid the splendours of Hyde-Park, more than once, while walking there); "Bread-and-water wages are refused *me* ["then, I used to say" *crossed out*], among these liberal allotments going. Unfair as possible;—perhaps unwise as possible too: but whom can I blame for it? No one, *and* everybody;—the plain import of which is silent submission to the fact. Well, I can finish this Book for the poor blind blockheads, fling it at their feet; then get a *rifle*, and to the Backwoods for good!" So, now & then; not often;—and always there was a practical whisper audible "This will never do, my friend!"—[178]

sailing over the ocean and burying himself in the remote backwoods of the American West. Yet he did not carry out the plan* and put it off at this

* never came near the length of 'plan.'

177. The *Foreign Quarterly Review*, not the *Foreign Review*, published his "Goethe's Works," in 10 (Aug. 1832), 1–44. The *New Monthly Magazine* published his "Death of Goethe," in 34 (June 1832), 507–512.

178. Cf. *Reminiscences*, I, 108; Froude, *Carlyle*, II, 477; III, 48; and Wilson, *Carlyle*, II, 408. Carlyle's letters of the mid-1830's occasionally take up the possibility of his emigrating to America.

time so that he might complete one more work to which he felt himself called: to set down in a history of the French Revolution his views on the political and social problems of the present, problems which the Revolution sought mightily to solve but which its followers had left behind uncompleted. For this, London offered the necessary literary resources, and for solitude and shelter from the confusion of daily life, where could he better satisfy his inclination for a secluded, solitary life than in the cosmopolitan bustle of London? Carlyle took up residence in Great Cheyne Row, a street in the southwestern suburb of Chelsea near the Thames, and in the house which he moved into at the time he lived[179] until he moved to Edinburgh.*

* [*Carlyle crosses out "he moved to Edinburgh" and writes:*] Never dreamt of "*übersiedel*ing" [*moving*] thither! It was a mad notion that rose on the Boys's appointing me their "Rector": "Here at last is a practical career for him" (strictly equal to *zero* in all senses): "why not remove to Edinburgh; & build us" (without clay or stubble) "such a University as never was!" said many newspapers and inconsiderate persons.

The articles on biography and on Boswell's *Life of Johnson* in *Fraser's Magazine* and an article entitled "Corn-Law Rhymes" in the *Edinburgh Review* give evidence of his interest during 1832 in the study of the present and of history.* In his article on biography he introduces a new

* at Craigenputtoch, all these.

mythical character à la Teufelsdröckh, Professor Gottfried Sauerteig, that gifted alter ego of Carlyle's who has since accompanied him in his literary career as his guardian spirit and occasionally even in the *History of Frederick the Great* is summoned from the Underworld when it becomes necessary to enliven the narrative with pithy and forceful expressions. In his first appearance, Sauerteig declared himself emphatically in favor of realism in the portrayal of a man's life—in other words, in favor of the historical, as opposed to the merely half-true, fictionalized biography, the form it always took. In his opinion, nothing compared in interest and significance with the full representation of the actual events of a man's life. The chief thing, Carlyle adds, is only that the actual events really happened and the biographer approach his work with "*an open loving*

179. Althaus (1869) changes "lived" to "still lives" and omits the rest of the sentence.

heart," [180] with the sole purpose of getting at the truth, not striving for effect. Boswell's *Life of Johnson* shows what might be achieved in this way. But unfortunately such biographies were, he believed, all too rare. We turn over "those old interminable Chronicles ... or still worse," we patiently examine

> those modern Narrations, of the Philosophic kind, where 'Philosophy, teaching by Experience,' has to sit like owl on housetop, *seeing* nothing, *understanding* nothing, uttering only, with such solemnity, her perpetual most wearisome *hoo-hoo*:—what hope have we, except the for most part fallacious one of gaining some acquaintance with our fellow-creatures, though dead and vanished, yet dear to us; how they got along in those old days, suffering and doing; to what extent, and under what circumstances, they resisted the Devil and triumphed over him, or struck their colours to him, and were trodden under foot by him; how, in short, the perennial Battle went, which men name Life, which we also in these new days, with indifferent fortune, have to fight, and must bequeath to our sons and grandsons to go on fighting. ... [No hope. ...] Your modern Historical Restaurateurs are indeed little better than high-priests of Famine; that keep choicest china dinner-sets, only no dinner to serve therein. [181]

Similar abrupt and peremptory judgments by Carlyle upon his predecessors and contemporaries in the writing of history recur often in his works. Inasmuch as history was for him above all a warm, vibrant and living account of the social conditions of mankind and its leading figures, no one can deny that his criticism was justified and that his own achievements in this field, compared with those of his contemporaries and predecessors, represented a higher ideal of historical writing. He also thought that Boswell's *Life of Johnson*, when seen from this perspective, merited the highest praise and the keenest study, all the more in that it brought into view a great, vigorous and heroic personality. He likewise praised in similar terms the "Corn-Law Rhymes," social and political poems by an iron-worker in Sheffield, as a remarkable creation of the times. A new mythical figure, Smelfungus Redivivus, the representative of literary parasitism and the exact opposite of Sauerteig, [182] opened the

180. "Biography," in *Works*, XXVIII, 57.
181. *Works*, XXVIII, 46–47. Althaus inserts the words in brackets.
182. Changed in Althaus (1869) to "Sauerteig's twin-brother."

discussion with some despairing remarks about the impossibility of keeping up critically with the overproduction of literature, especially in poetry. Yet with all due respect for such a high authority, Carlyle disagrees. The "Corn-Law Rhymes" would be worthy of attention, he believes, if it were only because they come from a so-called "uneducated" poet—indeed for that very reason—for from such humble origins one may in fact *a priori* expect more manly native power and more genuine unhypocritical feeling than from the sophisticated members of the upper classes. "Here," he cries out,

> is a voice coming from the deep Cyclopean forges, where Labour, in real soot and sweat, beats with his thousand hammers 'the red son of the furnace'; doing personal battle with Necessity, and her dark brute Powers, to make them reasonable and serviceable; an intelligible voice from the hitherto Mute and Irrational, to tell us at first-hand how it is with him, what in very deed is the theorem of the world and of himself, which he, in those dim depths of his, in that wearied head of his, has put together.[183]

Yet interest in obtaining at first hand information about these regions is not all.

> The great excellence of our Rhymer, be it understood, then, we take to consist even in this, often hinted at already, that he is *genuine*. Here is an earnest truth-speaking man; no theoriser, sentimentaliser, but a practical man of work and endeavour, man of sufferance and endurance. The thing that he speaks is not a hearsay, but a thing which he has himself known, and by experience become assured of. He has used his eyes for seeing; uses his tongue for declaring what he has seen. His voice, therefore, among the many noises of our Planet, will deserve its place better than the most; will be well worth some attention. Whom else should we attend to but such? The man who speaks with some half shadow of a Belief, and supposes, and inclines to think; and considers not with undivided soul, what is true, but only what is plausible, and will find audience and recompense: do we not meet him at every street-turning, on all highways and byways; is he not stale, unprofitable, ineffectual, wholly grown a weariness of the

183. *Works*, XXVIII, 138.

flesh? So rare is his opposite in any rank of Literature or of Life, so very rare, that even in the lowest he is precious.[184]

The preceding explanation gives us a glimpse into Carlyle's way of thinking and into his sincere concern to familiarize himself, at first hand and using the original sources, with present conditions and historical events—and to present in its own terms what is already well-known. Two essays written the following year (1833)* on Diderot and Cagliostro

* ditto.[185]

provide splendid examples of the astonishing industry and the brilliant powers of description with which he portrayed those theories in his own works. These essays, apparently studies for the intended* *History of the*

* no *intention* that way yet.[186]

French Revolution, are, however, of interest in their own right, apart from the *History*, as self-contained masterpieces of the historical portrait. In the biography of Diderot the whole world of the eighteenth-century Enlightenment, its philosophy and its work on the *Encyclopédie*, unfolds before our eyes. In the Cagliostro biography we see the chaotic world of his mysticism and his quackery. After all that we have said about Carlyle's position regarding the subversive, anti-idealistic tendencies of skepticism and materialism, we need not explain that he gave only partial recognition to Diderot and his associates on the *Encyclopédie*—and that only as representatives of a necessary transitional process in the intellectual development of their age. As to Cagliostro and the portion of mankind represented by him, he expressed only a rhadamanthian damnation. However, he agreed with the opinion of Sauerteig (whom we cite again), namely, that which declares the life of every man to be a poem which deserves to be read, even if it should turn out to be nothing more than a lampoon or a libel on mankind. "A flesh-and-blood Poem of the purest Pasquil sort"[187] is indeed the life of this Cagliostro, king of the quacks, liars and humbugs; and yet the exposure of the liar and the charlatan, the fraud and the fake along the lines of Cagliostro, is, for the liberation

184. Ibid., pp. 145–146.
185. As both the essays on Diderot and Cagliostro were published in 1833, Althaus assumes they were written in that year.
186. Only in late 1833 did Carlyle openly admit that he was thinking of writing a study of the French Revolution.
187. *Works*, XXVIII, 253. For Sauerteig's opinion, see p. 249.

of mankind and the victory of truth, as essential as the example of heroic acts. "Wholly despicable," declares Carlyle (and we encounter here the perfect formulation of another characteristic teaching of his philosophy, often repeated and restated), "at once detestable and forgetable," is

> but your half-knave, he who is neither true nor false; who never in his existence once spoke or did any true thing (for indeed his mind lives in twilight, with cat-vision, incapable of *discerning* truth); and yet had not the manfulness to speak or act any decided lie; but spent his whole life in plastering together the True and the False, and therefrom manufacturing the Plausible. Such a one our Transcendentals have defined as a Moral Hybrid and chimera; therefore, under the moral point of view, as an Impossibility, and mere deceptive Nonentity,—put together for commercial purposes. Of which sort, nevertheless, how many millions, through all manner of gradations, from the wielder of kings' sceptres to the vender of brimstone matches, at tea-tables, council-tables, behind shop-counters, in priests' pulpits, incessantly and everywhere, do now, in this world of ours, in this Isle of ours, offer themselves to view!
>
> From such, at least from this intolerable over-proportion of such, might the merciful Heavens one day deliver us! Glorious, heroic, fruitful for his own Time, and for all Time and all Eternity, is the constant Speaker and Doer of Truth! If no such again, in the present generation, is to be vouchsafed us, let us have at least the melancholy pleasure of beholding a decided Liar.[188]

Thus Cagliostro wanders over the earth before our eyes as the great hero of the lie and of humbug, and the great multitude—who believe him and applaud him—at the same time find in him their judgment. But Carlyle's intellect and descriptive powers are not restricted simply to vigorous adherence to these controlling points of view. He mastered the countless details of life just as well as he did his great conceptualizations. The human theater is created before us on a grand scale. Surrounded by the trappings of the age, dressed in its costumes, individual and dramatic as life itself, the characters stride across the stage of time, tragic and comic, great and small, each in his own way taking part in the unfolding of the drama. In fact, this Cagliostro-drama, in style and conception, quite takes on the character of the *History of the French*

188. Ibid., pp. 253–254.

Revolution, and in the context of Carlyle's literary career it should be considered, not merely as a study for it, but as a prologue to it.

During the next three years he was completely immersed in this great work which appeared in three volumes in 1837 under the title *The French Revolution: A History*, by Thomas Carlyle. It was the first time that he published a book under his own name, and this initial appearance before the public immediately secured national acclaim for the solitary sage of Chelsea. Although there were already many histories of the French Revolution, here was one which presented that world-shaking event in a totally new light. Indeed, no history like this one—with such poetic fire of imagination, magnificent vitality, and irresistible, overpowering humor and pathos—had ever been written before. Epic and history, drama and rhapsody, transcendental idealism and coarse realistic Dutch paintings of everyday life, penetrating insight into the hidden influences working upon characters and events, and a vast individual creative talent—all combined in a work of genius which did not merely retell the history of the Revolution but actually *reproduced* it. People were perplexed and dazzled by such an extraordinary creation, overcome by its power, resentful and indignant at its philosophical radicalism and the fearless revelation of the deep perception of the world and of man which they read on every page. However much the critics may have found fault with the spirit of the conception and the [189] diction modeled on Jean Paul, they were unanimous in acknowledging the genius and the magnitude of the work. Moreover, despite his deep conviction in regard to historical necessity and despite his admiring recognition of the world-shaking energy and effect of the Revolution, Carlyle was by no means one of those who glorified its victory, seeing it as the ultimate achievement, the last desirable result of the struggle for human freedom against human servitude. For him, its greatness lay in its role as the nemesis which mercilessly destroyed the rotten, the half-true, the untrue and the dead formulas of the past; it was, as well, the thunderstorm which cleared the heavy, dust-filled atmosphere of the century. Yet even more highly than these destructive powers, he cherished the creation of a new harmonious state of things which the Revolution had left uncompleted. The seething chaos of the *ancien régime* was torn apart in rough, powerful contrasts. But the god of the Revolution, like the ancient Saturn, consumed its

---

189. Althaus (1869) inserts "wonderful."

children, and the immense problem—how to create from the turbulent elements a world of freedom where men could live in dignity—remained unsolved. A great man appeared, to be sure, who ended the Revolution and reorganized the state. Yet despite his indisputable greatness this man was not the hero whom mankind could recognize as the founder of a new era in history. The Revolution ended, as Carlyle said,[190] with the whistle of Napoleon's bullets which struck down the last resistance of the radical revolutionaries, and with this he likewise ended his history.

Fraser's Magazine and the *Westminster Review* published this same year, as supplements and contributions to the *History of the French Revolution*, his articles on the diamond necklace incident,* on Mirabeau and on the

* written 4 or 5 years *before.*[191]

parliamentary history of the Revolution.* We mention them here,

* written *shortly after French Revolution.*—[192]

however, excellent as they are, only in passing as evidence of their author's tenacious and indefatigable industry. More interesting from a personal point of view is the fact that Carlyle during these very years, soon after the appearance of his history, made his début as a lecturer.* He

* was obliged to do it,—in spite of his detestation.

announced a course of six lectures on German literature,[193] and the elite of London society gathered in Willis's Rooms to see and hear the celebrated* author of the *History of the French Revolution. Sartor Resartus*

* alas!

now also appeared as a book under his name. His fame spread beyond the literary circles of his friends to an ever larger audience, and the great public, which until then had known little about Thomas Carlyle, gradually began to realize what an independent, brilliant seeker after truth and

190. *Works*, IV, 320. J. H. Rose disputes this point in his edition of Carlyle's history (London: George Bell, 1902), III, 379.

191. "The Diamond Necklace," written at Craigenputtoch in 1833, appeared in *Fraser's Magazine*, 15 (Jan. and Feb., 1837), 1–19, 172–189.

192. "Memoirs of Mirabeau" and the "Parliamentary History of the French Revolution," both written in 1836 after Carlyle had completed the first two of the three volumes of the *French Revolution*, appeared in the *London and Westminster Review*, 26 (Jan. 1837), 382–439, and 27 (April 1837), 233–247.

193. Not published. See Dyer, p. 131.

thinker lived in their midst. Those lectures, however, passed relatively unobserved* in the whirl of the season. Twelve lectures the following

* *kindest* **treatment they could have had, you may believe** *me*.

year (1838) on the history of European culture, given at the Marylebone Literary Institution,* caused a greater sensation. According to Leigh

* **long thick[?]** "*Lecture-Room*" **(the only** *sizable* **one that could be discovered), find that was rigorously all.**

Hunt's account in the *Examiner*, they developed a philosophy of history along the lines of the Germans. Not only their rich content but also the personality of the speaker brought out a most distinguished audience in the Institution's hall. A tall figure with a deadly serious, almost melancholy appearance stepped onto the speaker's platform. He was not a speaker in the ordinary sense of the word, but only an earnest man who was master of his subject, who stood on the firm ground of deep convictions which essentially dictated the form and impression of his lecture. His voice was soft and full and without strain, and he spoke to the large, intent audience as if he were speaking to a circle of friends around the home fireside. He had with him papers with notes on them; yet they seemed to hinder him. He soon put them aside and continued freely and fluently without other aid. "He . . . *extemporizes:* he does not read," Leigh Hunt wrote in the *Examiner*.

> We doubted, on hearing Monday's lecture, whether he would ever attain, in this way, the fluency as well as depth for which he ranks among celebrated talkers in private; but Friday's discourse relieved us. He 'strode away,' like Ulysses himself; and had only to regret, in common with his audience, the limits to which one hour gratified him.[194] The effect of hearty convictions like these, uttered in such simple, truthful words, and with the flavour of a Scottish accent (as if some Puritan had come to life again, liberalized by German philosophy, and his own intense reflections and experience) can be duly appreciated only by those who see it.[195]

194. *Examiner*, 6 May 1838, p. 278.
195. *Examiner*, 12 May 1839, p. 294. Hunt's *Examiner* accounts of Carlyle's lectures may be read in R. H. Shepherd, *Memoirs of the Life and Writings of Thomas Carlyle . . .* (London: W. H. Allen, 1881), I, 176-196. The lectures on the history of literature, not published during Carlyle's lifetime, appeared in 1892 in two editions, both based on the detailed notes which Thomas Chisholm Anstey took of all but one of them. See Dyer, pp. 131-133.

Thus Carlyle appeared to his listeners at that time, a man all of a piece, to whom it made no difference whether he came forward as a solitary thinker in his study or as a speaker before a large and eminent gathering, whose only concern was the free presentation of his ideas, and who thus and in no other way would and could speak as the spirit moved him. And if we leap from these lectures of thirty years ago to his recent address as Rector in Edinburgh, where—seventy years old, serious, venerable, gray-haired but still erect—he presented himself in the same way before the new generation of young people, and once more put aside the traditional practice of a written speech and trusted to the inspiration of the moment, we cannot help admiring such a creative and active spirit, such a grand unity and purposefulness of character, however differently we may judge several of the unconventional paths into which his thinking led him. Let us immediately add here that Carlyle's activities as a lecturer were attributable less to his own personal inclination than to the pressure of his friends, in part* also probably from the necessities of his financial

* im ganzen, ja einzig [*on the whole, indeed the only*]!

situation. For as stoically and simply as he lived and as diligently as he worked,[196] he was in terms of the demands of living in London still a relatively poor man, a man moreover who had to worry not only about himself alone. It would have also been easy for him, if he had been so inclined, to earn a very good living as lecturer, as was done later with relative ease by one of his great* contemporaries, Thackeray, with whom

* oh, dear!

he had much in common and who died at an early age. But he did not like to appear before large gatherings and took little satisfaction in the applause they bestowed on him. Requests that he repeat his lectures in other English cities were thus turned down, and the courses already mentioned were followed by just two others: in 1839 lectures on the revolutions of modern Europe,[197] and in 1840 the most famous of all,* the

* , being the *only printed* set. As to '*berühmt*' [*famous*], don't speak of it all! My Public was so dark & vacant; wonderstruck at the light of a lucifer match.

196. Changed in Althaus (1869) to "For stoically simple as he lived and untiringly diligent as he worked."

197. See Dyer, p. 133, and the fragmentary reports of this lecture series preserved in the *Examiner*, which are reprinted in Shepherd's *Carlyle* (cited in note 195), I,

197–201. Interleaved between pp. 8 and 9 of Althaus's biography of Carlyle is a sheet approximately 8″ × 6″ entitled "Lecture I" on which Carlyle has written on both sides in what is clearly an earlier hand. It contains what may be a draft of or his notes for a first lecture in this series which he later rejected and which he may never have delivered before an audience. Hunt's report in the *Examiner* of 5 May 1839 confirms that it was not the actual first lecture. The notes succinctly indicate the main lines of Carlyle's attitude toward revolution and reveal as well from what scanty materials he could hold forth for an hour or more.

Lecture I.

REVOLUTIONS our habitual state for these last 3 centuries. Hatefulness of them; necessity of them: expansion by *shoots*. Systole diastole. All hatred at first; all found at test to have meant something just important and desirable. For us in the struggle and doubt we live in, difficult to conceive harmony and faith. "Independence." Every original man a revolution. define an original man as one that does *not* go by hearings, must verify his hearings[.] Progress of the species: what? 3 revolutions related in the way of paternity and filiation. Order the *necessity* for man. Time, mortality; love of chance, yet perseverance[.] Be useful to take a view *of Europe* as it was[.]

IMMIGRATIONS lasted nearly 2 centuries (375—568 Lombards). History slims it over.

LOVE OF ORDER inherent in man. NOTHING CAN BE ETERNAL; yet many things always thought to be so: here is the root of an endless struggle.

HABIT foundation of order: Kings and nobles were found *useful*; Priests and Popes did yield spiritual edification.

JACQUERIE (better read about that) was an attempt at revolution *without* a faith? Every revolution has a faith. Not men hard usage will produce a revolution; tho' "oppression will drive a wise man *mad*."

All revolutions blamed at first, all found at last to have meant something. It is not physical hardship that alone rouses men, but the thought withal (and the faith) that such hardship is UNJUST.

LOYALTY deepest want of man (perhaps). Boswell Johnson. Not lands or money or the kind review of never so many people that makes one *rich*: it is the friends[.]

NECESSITY OF UTTERING ONESELF: effort of all men to see shaped externally to them the thing they have in them as a thought. Not a hut one builds but &c— steam ship. SPEECH itself, according to C.—CHURCH originated in this—we all have a kind of secret church. Beautify what we love &c (in reference to Church).

ALL Revolutions are of religious character: originate in *right*, that is, or that is thought to be, will of God.— Parent, child, events are? Rather river and brooks running into it.

LEGISLATORS-*tendencies* merely motivated by them. Plant struggling thro' stones; they lift off the stones.

LAISSEZ FAIRE: Nobody's, not even anybody's slave. Burns, poor man seeking work. No horse is in that state.

DUTY AND THE SLAVE: stand silent over both of them. "Conflux of two Eternities": "waited an eternity," very strange to consider at any time: immensity, the contrary of it *not* conceivable; stupidity saves us (hinders us) from thinking of these things.

lectures on hero-worship. This latest and last course made far and away the greatest impression and was also the only one which Carlyle published. Any one reading these historical-biographical sketches, rich in ideas and artistically constructed, would find it difficult not to believe that Carlyle in this instance did depart from his habit of extemporizing. It remains a fact however that the lectures on hero-worship were given exactly as they were published;[198] and if proof is needed that Carlyle speaks as he writes, that his style is no assumed manner but rather was and is the natural expression of his way of thinking, simple reference to these lectures would suffice to dispel suspicions. What distinguishes them from his other works is a certain mellowness of tone, a certain moderation in the[199] gruffness and manner of presentation, wherein one may recognize an involuntary effect of the hearers upon the speaker. Perhaps this circumstance contributed its share to the extraordinary popularity which the published book has enjoyed. But the train of thought and the basis of his way of seeing things remain the same. Indeed, we find here the perfect formulation of his view of the historical development of mankind,[200] namely that its real progress and sole health are attributable to the deeds and the example of a chosen group of heroic personalities (a view which frequently runs counter to the democratic *Zeitgeist*) carried out to its fullest extent.[201] We exist to emulate and revere them. The task and goal of mankind was thus proclaimed in these terms: not to strive for mastery but rather to obey the masters chosen by destiny; not to doubt and criticize but rather to revere the gospel of great men as a revelation of the divine and to work in its service; not to aspire to the fulfilment of earthly happiness but rather to subordinate all personal desires and claims to the general necessity. Upon the success of general causes and effects he placed the least emphasis; instead he put direct stress upon the creative activity of those who by God's grace were the great leaders and thinkers. These heroes, he explained, not only expressed the thoughts

198. The title page of the first edition reveals that Carlyle published his lectures with considerable (though not major) "Emendations and Additions."

199. Althaus (1869) inserts "Jean-Paulian."

200. Changed in Althaus (1869) to "It was quite specific in the perfect characterization, already mentioned several times previously, of his view of the historical development of mankind."

201. The clause in parentheses is omitted in Althaus (1869) and the rest of the sentence changed to "which he carried out to the fullest extent in the lectures on hero-worship."

of their age but also revealed its secret gospel; they acted not only as instruments of their age but also embodied creatively the eternal logic of things. All spheres of life thus have their heroes to show. We see Odin the hero as divinity, Mohammed the hero as prophet, Dante and Shakespeare the hero as poet, Luther and Knox the hero as priest, Johnson, Rousseau and Burns the hero as man of letters, Cromwell and Napoleon the hero as king. Our levelling age also harasses the hero. If there still is any hope for the inspired hero-worshipper in the restless chaotic pressures for the rebirth of a now-crumbling world, it is that even today the capacity of the human heart for hero-worship remains unextinguished and that even for us a saving hero is ordained.

His essay *Chartism*, published in 1839, had preceded the lectures on hero-worship. Its subject was the social situation in England, especially the problem of pauperism. In it, Carlyle depicts in the most somber colors the wretched conditions of the present and finds much to censure, little or nothing to praise, in the efforts of leading public figures to deal with the prevailing misery. Just to cure this disease called for a great and inspired mind which would scorn mere palliatives. The popular principle of laissez-faire seemed to him most contemptible of all. The ignorant had, he believed, an inalienable right to be led by the wise, and when the moment comes to act it is of infinitely greater importance to pay attention to practical forces than to so-called human rights. The prerogatives of Parliament may be great, but necessity and natural laws are greater. Indeed, he declared in the chapter entitled "Mights and Rights" that, basically, might was right.[202] However sharply these two may conflict with one another from moment to moment, if one simply gives them time they will come in the end to be recognized as one. The reader will have no difficulty in finding in this maxim another expression of the famous principle of Hegel's philosophy of law, namely, that what is reality is rational, except that Carlyle has this maxim apply not to the present but to the future,* and thus uses it to justify a masterful *coup*

* What floods of nonsense have been and are spoken & thought (what they call thinking) about this poor maxim of Carlyle's! C. had discovered for himself, not without a satisfaction of religious kind, that no man who is not in the *right*, were he even a Napoleon I at the head of armed Europe, has any real *might* whatever, but

202. See *Works*, XXIX, 146–147, and cf. pp. 173–174.

will at last be found *might*less, and to have *done*, or settled as a fixity, nothing at all, except precisely so far as he was *not* in the wrong. Abolition and erosion awaits all 'doings' of his, except just what part of them *was right*. He chains Europe under his feet perhaps, beneath the stars is nothing so great, &c &c: but wait, you, till the *Books* (of Heaven's Chancery) are fully made up, and the accounts *settled*: what was true and right of your Napoleon's doings is acknowledged & remains *done* to all times and eternities; what was not true and *right* (or *accordant* with God Almighty's doings and appointings ["laws" *crossed out*]) is found not to be *done* at all, but *mis*done or *un*done (and to have begun, on the instant, to be *expunged* and *annihilated* again, often a long & painful process),—with all the *damages* accurately charged, too. And your great Napoleon, openly *bankrupt* under that latter clause, is flung out to the nettles and broken bottles; & the salutary process of *expunction* goes on to the end, as fast as it can. So that *right* and *might* are identical, in the long run; glory to Heaven!— Upon which many men of weak judgment take to wondering, and not a few to exclaiming, "Ha, Carlyle thinks might is right, the scandalous fellow-mortal!" And hate the poor man, more or less; which is of no consequence: but for themselves it is a dismal pity that they, and all men, don't *believe* on that point, with their whole soul, as Carlyle believes,—which so few of the Conspicuous of mankind seem to do!— Does *Bismarck* perhaps? With very sincere joy, I sometimes think so, latterly; and if so, since Wellington and Peel died (& *they* were not first-rate examples), he is a Unique in the world to me.[203]

d'état, a heroic usurpation and domination of the existing order. Under all circumstances this is a dangerous, double-edged* principle, and, as one

* no: if you understand it, it is very strictly a 'one-edged.'

203. A statement of fundamental importance which, in effect, speaks for itself and succeeds better than Carlyle's apologists in refuting the assertions of those— among them, Herbert Grierson, Eric Bentley, and a host of Nazi theorists—who accuse Carlyle of precipitating twentieth-century ills. Carlyle also took up the "might vs. right" concept in several of his major works: see, e.g., *Works*, III, 211; V, 242; X, 12; XI, 192. He may later have modified his opinion of Bismarck. See Wilson, *Carlyle*, VI, 439.

can well imagine, doubly repugnant to a people like the English so jealously proud of their ancient birthright of freedom. In fact, few of Carlyle's political and social teachings have encountered such violent opposition as has this doctrine of the unity of might and right, and no other of his beliefs could have more well-founded* objections raised

* oh none [*word illegible*]!

against it. *From a philosophical point of view it is surely clear that the

* Of all this, to end of paragraph, I know nothing: empty babble to me every line of it (under favour of Althaus)!—

present is the necessary consequence of the total historical process and that freedom in its highest sense is identical with necessity. However, as to the absolute value and the actual relationship between right and might as seen in the noblest dictatorship, i.e., that of Cromwell or of Napoleon, men's opinions are and will remain just as divided as they are over the extent to which one recognizes the reasonableness of the present situation. Even if the sense of hero-worship can survive in our levelling age and even if the hero to come can be sure of its admiration and its love, still nothing seems clearer than that the age expects less from the exercise of absolute rule by individual men than it does from the gradual dissemination and realization of humane principles, and that its hope is not only in the beneficent dictatorship but also in the undisputed freedom of nations. The rule of the silent—and silence imposing—Emperor of the French* shows what a benign dictatorship can do in our time. The

* what a pity *he* didn't in some small measure know C's doctrine, and practice it! 204

recent history of the North American republic reveals what a nation can achieve when guided by great principles; its deeds of heroism* compare

* Ach Gott! 205

204. Carlyle thought little of Napoleon III (1808–1873), Emperor of the French from 1852 until his forced abdication in 1870. He had met the "Copper Captain" (as he called him) in the late 1840's when he was still in exile in England.

205. Carlyle expressed his low opinion of the American North in "*Ilias (Americana) in Nuce*" (*American Iliad in a Nutshell*), first published in *Macmillan's Magazine*, 8 (Aug. 1863), 301. According to Moncure D. Conway, Carlyle later admitted that he had taken "the wrong side during the great struggle for the abolition of slavery in the United States, not because his sympathies were with the oppressors, but because he was misled as to the facts of the case by the stories told him by slave-owners concerning their patriarchal Arcadias in the South" (Henry J. Nicoll, *Thomas Carlyle* [Edinburgh: Macniven & Wallace, 1881], p. 198, citing Conway).

with the most famous deeds of Cromwell and Napoleon, and victory was achieved without subjecting the nation to the danger of a dictatorship. Particularly, as far as pauperism and the lack of existing social resources are concerned, it is evident that even the most high-minded dictator would not be in a position to rectify—either by his edicts or even by the best ordinances in the world—these consequences of deep-seated, widespread and complex causes and effects. Even Carlyle finally had to concede that improvement could be expected only through the slow working out of time; and in view of the way things are he recommends universal education and emigration as the only effective way to overcome pauperism.

It was an exciting time in England, a time of burning agitation on all contemporary social and political[206] problems. Carlyle, once launched upon this troubled sea, absorbed himself for years in contemplating these problems and investigating their historical background in the period of the English Revolution. *Chartism* was followed in 1843 by *Past and Present.* In this book Carlyle draws a profound parallel, full of pathos and poetry, between, on the one hand, the energetic, purposeful, self-confident work of men in former times including, by way of example, a detailed description of one Abbot Samson, head of the Abbey of Bury St. Edmunds in the thirteenth century, and, on the other, the skeptical, hesitating, ineffective activity of social and political leaders of the present-day. There in that far-distant world he sees the ideals of ordered cosmic action, here in the present nothing but decadence and chaotic disorder. Instead of adhering to divine laws, the present generation, he explains, respects no principles other than that of the greatest good and of parliamentary propriety. Its highest good is the gospel of Mammon; indeed, money transactions constitute the only tie between one person and another. Shameless do-nothingism in deed and say-nothingism in word; a game-preserving aristocracy unsullied by any kind of work; a working aristocracy sunk in ignoble service to Mammon; an idle aristocracy with yellowing parchments and arrogant absurdities—these and countless other evils press heavily upon us and bewilder our thoughts and actions. What a contrast between Oliver Cromwell and Sir Jabesh Windbag! Nonetheless, let us not lose heart. This England, despite her theorizings and platitudes, what a quantity of commonsense is to be found in her!—of all nations the stupidest in speech, the wisest in

---

206. Althaus (1869) omits "and political."

action.[207] Indeed, the world has only one monster: the lazy man who has accomplished nothing. An eternal nobility dwells in all work and*

*[*Carlyle crosses out "and" and writes after "blessed"*] der [*he who*].[208]

blessed is he who has found work. He asks no other blessing. Man does not need a new religion (what an amazing idea it is to want to discover a new god)*; still, it is probable that he will get one. The only true liturgy

*[*Opposite this sentence Carlyle writes:*] baddish Abstract, all this.

is a prayer for work. Indeed, it is great, and no other greatness compares to making a small piece of the Creation a little more productive, or making two human hearts a little wiser, more manly, happier—this is work for a god.[209] This so-called "Gospel of Work" is of special interest as complementing the view expressed in the chapter on "Mights and Rights," and to do Carlyle's philosophy justice one should bear both constantly in mind. A related train of thought led him from his admiration of great, manifest and world-shaking heroism to the glorification of the silent, hidden heroism of patient work. He viewed as noble, magnificent and worthy of reverence that hero who stirs up the world and shapes its destiny. But just as entitled to esteem and reverence and as happy is the unknown man who fulfils the world in himself and, in courageous struggle and renunciation, contributes his grain of sand to the great structure of the Eternities.[210]

While Carlyle was writing *Past and Present*, he was also preoccupied with the preparation of a great historical work: the editing of Cromwell's letters and speeches. It appeared in 1845 in four volumes.[211] If until then

207. Cf. *Works*, X, 160, and XXIX, 383. Althaus and Carlyle allude to Goethe's comment under 24 February 1825 in the *Conversations of Goethe with Eckermann and Soret*, trans. John Oxenford (London: George Bell, 1874), p. 116.

208. Carlyle alters Althaus's text to allude to *Faust* I, l. 1573, which he echoes in the "The Everlasting No" of *Sartor*: "Almost since earliest memory I had shed no tear; or once only when I, murmuring half-audibly, recited Faust's Death-song, that wild *Selig der den er im Siegesglanze findet* (Happy whom *he* finds in Battle's splendour) ..." (Harrold, *Sartor*, p. 165).

209. Althaus (1869) begins the next sentence with "That approximately was the train of thought of this new work, and."

210. Cf. *Works*, X, 67: "the grand still mirror of Eternity."

211. The first edition appeared in two volumes, the second in three; the "Third Edition, enlarged" (1850) was the first to appear in four volumes.

the extreme radicalism with which this great thinker condemned present conditions left the general public and the critics no other grounds for complaint than the strange, fantastic speech in which he expressed his ideas, admiration was universal for this truly magnificent presentation of the period and of the life and character of its greatest hero, Cromwell. He had thrown himself body and soul into a task which he regarded destiny had imposed upon him and in which he felt as if he were secretly in the world of his ideal. Puritanism, the Revolution, and Cromwell's dictatorship in which both culminated, were for him the last heroic epoch of English history. It struck him not only as most urgent but also as worthy of his most diligent efforts to further general understanding of this epoch before it faded away completely and perished under the "avalanche of Human Stupidity,"[212] which had already buried it beneath the refuse of hypocritical sentiments that alone remained. How he viewed earlier histories of the period and how he construed his task, he explained characteristically in the introduction under the heading "Anti-Dryasdust." This new mythical figure of Dryasdust, originally Sir Walter Scott's creation,[213] has in the meantime become familiar to the German reader in the *History of Frederick the Great*.[214] The simple recollection that in him Carlyle chastises the dry scholarly pedant, who in his concern for the exterior apparatus of history forgets its inner life, can accordingly suffice as explanation. The history of Puritanism had until then, he believed, been left to the arid, barren pedantry of the Dryasdusts. "All past Centuries," he said

> have rotted down, and gone confusedly dumb and quiet, even as that Seventeenth is now threatening to do. Histories are *as* perfect as the Historian is wise, and is gifted with an eye and a soul! For the leafy blossoming Present Time springs from the whole Past, remembered and unrememberable, so confusedly as we say:—and truly the Art of History, the grand difference between a Dryasdust and a sacred Poet, is very much even this: To distinguish well what does still reach to the surface, and is alive and frondent for us; and

212. *Works*, VI, 4–5.

213. Scott dedicates *Ivanhoe* (1819) to the Rev. Dr. Dryasdust of York, who also introduces several of his other novels. The original was John Croft (1732–1820), a well-known antiquary in York, a writer of small works, and something of an eccentric. For Carlyle's meeting with Croft, see *CL*, I, 283.

214. See, e.g., *Works*, XII, 319, and XIII, 342.

what reaches no longer to the surface, but moulders safe underground, never to send forth leaves or fruit for mankind any more: of the former we shall rejoice to hear; to hear of the latter will be an affliction to us; of the latter only Pedants and Dullards, and disastrous *male*factors to the world, will find good to speak. By wise memory and by wise oblivion: it lies all there! Without oblivion, there is no remembrance possible.[215]

And as the "sacred Poet," Carlyle raised up before the eyes of the present generation that seventeenth century—with its conflicts and sufferings, its events and personages—from the distant realm of shades of the past to a living, historical form. Cromwell's letters and speeches constituted only the thread which indicated the way through the labyrinth of events, the core around which contemporary history shaped itself: they were full of character, sparkling, and stirred by the surging stream of the age and its ideas. To say that history was gathered together with exemplary thoroughness, sifted critically, arranged within chronological sequence, and unified through an excellent commentary (though without doubt an enterprise demanding no slight acumen and no ordinary talent) would be only to express the most superficial praise to which this wonderful work can lay claim. Carlyle did much more. Under the magic wand of his genius that whole moribund world blossoms around us just as it once did. We breathe its air, we tread on its soil and earth; its shapes and colors, its costumes and landscape figures, its genre-paintings and biographical sketches give us a sense of intimacy as in a Dutch local color painting. What is more, we feel ourselves irresistibly transported back to its faith and its way of thinking, its destiny and its deeds. It is just as if we were not modern descendants, divided from them by a gulf of two hundred years of history, but rather contemporaries of those men and parties, the Roundheads and the Cavaliers, the Independents and the Levellers, the Long Parliament and the Protectorate, Charles I and Cromwell. Carlyle's language too, with its biblical severity and wealth of imagery, with its archaic and curious idioms and expressions, seems in secret harmony with its venerable subject. We come to believe we are hearing the speech of the age itself and feel as if the Puritan *Zeitgeist* itself were telling its history. There is no higher level for historical writing to achieve, and seldom does it succeed to such an extent. Looking back upon his portrayal

215. *Works*, VI, 7–8.

of the French Revolution, just as magnificent in its way, we find it difficult to decide perhaps which of the two works is the finer one. Yet if the goal of historical writing is to show the unity of idea and reality, of form and spirit, we might be tempted to declare this history of Cromwell the most perfect of Carlyle's historical works, since in it he presented not only historical reality but also a reality in harmony with his own ideals.

After such a monumental achievement he had a right to rest a while on his laurels. Five years passed before he again spoke to his contemporaries. Five eventful years,* filled with the Irish famine and the exodus

* Various Newspaper Sallies (in *Examiner* chiefly, in *Spectator* one or two[216]) fall in this epoch—not quite of idleness, tho' idler than it should have been, but of groping uncertainty on what was next to be done.[217] Boundless disgust of anarchies, Irish & other; not as yet utter despair of *Parliaments* for mending it,—not quite, till after Sir R. Peel's death. A good deal of acquaintance made with English Aristocracy (I do believe, in its selectest specimens), and some insight into it got.[218] *Hope* in "the revolutions of 1848" Carlyle never had; and any poor *joy* they gave him was as new proofs of the bankruptcy of Sham.

from Ireland, the revolutions in continental Europe, not to mention other lesser occurrences. Always an extremely sensitive observer of contemporary events, Carlyle followed the course of these movements with the deepest interest, the development of the Irish problem with bitter indignation, and the Revolutions of 1848 at first with cheerfully enthusiastic hope. Even for Germany he had hope, and from within the circle of his German friends in London where Germany's situation was being discussed, there rang out then even from his lips the cry: Long live the German Fatherland.* But he had hoped so fervently that he was deeply dis-

* "*Deutsche Vaterland*"—alas, that was his wish and prophecy always; but, at that time, seemed shoved quite over the horizon.[219]

216. Most of these "Newspaper Sallies" are republished in *Rescued Essays of Thomas Carlyle*, ed. Percy Newberry (London: The Leadenhall Press, [1892]).
217. Cf. Carlyle's Journal entry of 9 February 1848 in Froude, *Carlyle*, III, 421.
218. Carlyle probably has in mind here the Ashburtons.
219. Neuberg was one of those German friends with whom Carlyle discussed the 1848 revolution. See Althaus, "Erinnerungen," p. 827, and cf. Carlyle's letter to Neuberg of 23 August 1866 in (Thomas Sadler), "Carlyle and Neuberg," *Macmillan's Magazine*, 50 (Aug. 1884), 295.

appointed over the dismal failure of the revolutionary movement. After a brief, inspiring time of elation, the world again seemed to him to sink back into hopeless stagnation. It had proved nothing except its lack of universal and creative energy, and the longed-for heroic age of the leadership by the best and wisest seemed pushed further away than ever before. From this most disillusioned* and despairing state of mind there

* '*Enttäuscht*,' no, not a whit; but right heavy of heart, & growing ever heavier, he had long been.

came forth during 1849 and 1850 the celebrated *Latter-Day Pamphlets*. They first appeared, as the title indicates, in the form of pamphlets; afterward they were collected into a book and caused a sensation greater, perhaps, than any other which the political and social discourses of this idealistic thinker, teacher and critic of his age had caused. Not even in the essay on chartism had he summed up his own particular views on the shortcomings and needs of the present with such towering anger, caustic bitterness and reckless radicalism. His grim Dantesque depiction of the conditions of a decadent world, his prophetic anathema against its sins of commission and omission rang forth like a harsh dissonance in an age which basked in the splendor of a great and increasing prosperity and which was preparing one of the most significant cultural events of recent history, the first international exhibition of 1851. The *Latter-Day Pamphlets* included in their merciless verdict of damnation the labors and goals of every one of the existing parties, the institutions, the modes of thought, life and action of all ruling powers of state and society. No one but a great leader, nothing but the might which right represented, a true king and dictator (this was the general train of thought) could save or create out of this dreadful chaos a universe worthy of man.

An "Occasional Discourse on the Negro Question," the first of the series of pamphlets, immediately threw a glaring light on the relentless determination with which Carlyle sought to justify his dogma of the equality of might with right even in its most far-reaching implications. The pamphlet is nothing more nor less than a pitying shrug of the shoulders over the false philanthropy which brought about the emancipation of the slaves in the English colonies. The Negro, according to the author, once belonged to an inferior race, had therefore an inalienable right to be ruled by the more intelligent race, in this case the whites, will always misuse the freedom given him, and only in lasting dependency will enjoy that measure of happiness and freedom of which by the nature of things he is capable. Old-style slavery seems of course to Carlyle no less unjust than emancipation; but it should be transformed into being "hired for life,"[220] in other words, the conditions of medieval serfdom and bondage (which were best suited to their nature) should be restored among the blacks. A strange doctrine from a humane thinker like Carlyle! —a doctrine with which among modern philosophers, as he admitted, he found himself in a minority of one, but to which he nonetheless clung with the most resolute conviction. From this viewpoint the American Civil War likewise later appeared to him as a regrettable event, and this extraordinary phenomenon thus confirms to us the truth of the old cliché to the effect that opposites attract: a Carlyle who makes common cause with the "enlightened" defenders of the enslavement "ordained by nature" of whole classes of mankind. It is not surprising that a prologue along these lines did not exactly dispose his countrymen to respond favorably to the positions which he set forth in the remaining pamphlets and which had particular reference to England.

The next pamphlet "The Present Time" took the present in general as its theme and declared in essence that "British industrial existence seems fast becoming one huge poison-swamp of reeking pestilence";[221] that the British constitution as an ideal was incomplete and unworthy of completion;[222] that the study of society was actually the study of misfortune;[223] that beyond that an "Organisation of Labour" was needed,[224] but above all a king. Another pamphlet "Model Prisons" condemned the sickening philanthropy of present prison administration, which has no other result than the "drilling" of a "Devil's regiment of the line" made up of the "thriftless sweepings of creation."[225] A third "Downing Street" is directed against political administration, in which the author sees nothing but a wretched system of bewildering routine, "a world-wild

---

220. *Works*, XXIX, 368, and elsewhere in the essay. "The Negro Question" is not formally one of the *Latter-Day Pamphlets* but a "precursor" (Carlyle's term, ibid., p. 349). In 1853 he published the essay independently as "Occasional Discourse on the Nigger Question."

221. Ibid., XX, 27.

222. Cf. ibid., pp. 30–32.

223. Cf. ibid., pp. 44–45.

224. Cf. ibid., p. 46.

225. Ibid., pp. 56–59, for these phrases, extrapolated by Althaus from several pages of Carlyle's essay.

jungle . . . inhabited by doleful creatures, deaf or nearly so to human reason and entreaty."[226] A great statesman should take their place, or the ten best men chosen from a people of twenty-seven millions; for the only true democracy is one in which qualified men, wherever found, are at the head. In the following pamphlet "New Downing Street" he takes up the same subject and discusses the conditions necessary to bring about a significant improvement. "Our Public Life and our Private, our State and our Religion" in their present condition were nothing but "a tissue of half-truths and whole-lies."[227] The need above all needs was the eradication of pauperism, our great social sin,[228] and government by men capable of bringing about the realization of the good. "He is a good man that can command and obey: he that cannot is a bad."[229] It is thus essential to teach the rising generation to acquire these fundamental virtues. Unfortunately, the present system of education offers nothing but "broken crumbs of mere *speech*"; "what if our next set of Souls'-Overseers were to be *silent* ones very mainly?"[230] This line of thought leads him in the next pamphlet "Stump Orator" to renew his old opposition to the evil tendency in our age to talk too much. Nothing but words, words, words everywhere. The whole world pays homage to the "Moloch" of "public speaking," "parliamentary eloquence"[231]—and intellectual death is the consequence. Indeed, it might be that a benevolent "plan of reform for our benighted world" "could appoint at least one generation to pass its life in silence."[232] "If such a plan were practicable, how the chaff might be winnowed out of every man, and out of all human things!"[233] "Be not a Public Orator, thou brave young British man!" "To speak, or to write, Nature did not peremptorily order thee; but to work she did!"[234]

It is hardly surprising that Carlyle, seeing things the way he did, had little good to say of Parliament. Parliament, he declared in the following

226. Ibid., p. 87.
227. Ibid., p. 160.
228. Cf. ibid., pp. 158, 164, 166. "Pauperism" is Carlyle's term for "unemployment."
229. Ibid., p. 167.
230. Ibid., pp. 167, 168.
231. Ibid., p. 212.
232. Ibid., p. 209.
233. Ibid., p. 210.
234. Ibid., p. 212.

pamphlet, is useless the way it is, and it is useless to attempt its reform. It does nothing but talk and cast votes and even that "*not* very much in earnest." Only two parliaments enjoyed true sovereignty: the English Long Parliament and the French Convention. The greatest problem "is not a more and more perfectly elected Parliament" like the present one, "but some reality of a Ruling Sovereign to preside over Parliament." "The mass of men consulted at hustings, upon any high matter whatsoever, is as ugly an exhibition of human stupidity as this world sees." "Could you entirely exclude the slave's vote, and admit only the heroic free man's vote," then "the ultimate New Era, and best possible condition of human affairs, had actually come."[235] In the meantime, however, as the next pamphlet "Hudson's Statue" explains, there is no hope for the imminent onset of this golden age—inasmuch as the heroes now are not Cromwell but rather Hudson, king of the railways, and countless other demi-gods. According to the last pamphlet "Jesuitism," this general deterioration, falseness and hypocrisy have finally forced their way into the realm of art. "Here too, as elsewhere, the consummate flower of Consecrated Unveracity reigns supreme."[236] The new Houses of Parliament are nothing but "a wilderness of stone pepperboxes";[237] "all the Fine Arts" are transacted in "after-dinner amusements."[238] "Surely this ignoble sluggishness, sceptical torpor . . . is not doomed to be" our final "natural state. . . . Under this brutal stagnancy there lies painfully imprisoned some tendency which could become heroic."[239]

This, in a few broad strokes, is the train of thought in the *Latter-Day Pamphlets*. One should reflect upon these ideas as presented and developed in Carlyle's stern, powerful language in which his own intelligence and thought abound; and upon the realities which he subjects to his criticism and which are set off by the wonderful light of his characteristic and allegorical plurals: Eternities, Immensities, Silences, Veracities on the one hand, Trivialities, Loquacities, Unveracities, and Shams on the other. If one ponders these matters, one can gain an impression of the impact which his Puritan lectures of reprimand must have produced

---

235. Althaus reflects Carlyle's arguments and ideas in "Parliaments." See ibid., pp. 214, 225, 226, 228, 233, 242, 250.
236. Ibid., p. 320.
237. Ibid., p. 321.
238. Ibid., p. 328.
239. Ibid., p. 335.

upon the latter-day generation for which they were intended. In fact, they attacked not only the spokesman for laissez-faire, for materialism and for sly "vulpine intellect,"[240] whose ways of thinking Carlyle parodied in the last of his pamphlets by a system—sketched with grim humor—of "Pig-Philosophy,"[241] but also the noble humane thinkers. In general, we may justifiably protest that he confused ends and means and did not do justice to the unavoidable necessity of slow historical growth. But the *Latter-Day Pamphlets*, precisely because of their great measure of idealism raised to the highest degree and their impassioned single-mindedness, played an important role in the stimulating impact which was to some extent inherent in all of Carlyle's works. Each pamphlet is a genuine storehouse filled with seed corn of the future. As the stern sower reaches into his full sack and scatters the seeds, it seems almost impossible that not a single one of these would sink deeply into the seed-field of time, into the hearts and minds of all readers, and move them to serious reflection and high-minded resolves. Carlyle himself wrote these pamphlets at a time of great mental and spiritual distress. His oppressive thoughts had weighed upon him like a bad dream, and even after he had externalized these problems he felt weary and exhausted from the dust and heat of conflict. It was a relief for him to begin another work, this time a work of reminiscence—the life of his friend John Sterling. It is also a work full of serious, brooding reflections, but in tone and attitude quite different from the *Latter-Day Pamphlets*. No longer is the prophet heard prophesying in the temple of the unknown God, nor the judge delivering to a corrupt age a verdict of damnation. Rather, one sees Carlyle the man, walking with men through life, sensitively sharing their joys and sorrows, and presenting in the earthly pilgrimage of his friend, as if in the course of a conversation, a glimpse of contemporary history. Perhaps in no other book does his portrait come before us so intimately and directly, and no other was so rapidly and easily written. Its completion—the book came out in 1851—was also a welcome event for the reason that it gave him the peace of mind needed to undertake a great historical work which from then until the recent present was to claim his undivided attention: the *History of Frederick the Great*.

In 1852 Carlyle laid out the plan for this last and most extensive of his works. He had reached his fifty-seventh year, but felt, in spite of his not

240. Cf. ibid., pp. 128, 185.
241. In "Jesuitism," pp. 315–318.

infrequent ill-health, that he was still quite able to carry out so extensive a work.* What moved him to choose this subject is readily evident on

* no great feeling of that; but a great need & determination to *try*.

recalling the fundamental orientation in his philosophy of human life and the subjects of his previous historical studies.[242] In fact, his historical works are related to each other as characteristically* as are the social and

* *French Revolution*, explosion of Sham-kings into Tartarus; *Friedrich II*, delineation of a *True King*, in modern guise: one's first work and one's last;—and the *Ille ego* [*I am he who*] &c (of Virgil)[243] partly *humming* itself within one. For the rest, a Work some hundreds of times more difficult than, in my lazy and inconsiderate *haste*, I had ever thought it would be. Dim *feeling* of that terrible truth I had always, in the background; but shoved it over, careless fellow, & strode on to the attack. I was in miserable health, too.— Enough.[244]

philosophical speculations in *Chartism, Past and Present* and the *Latter-Day Pamphlets*. In *The French Revolution*, his first historical work, he had

242. Althaus (1869) begins the next sentence with "For even though these latter may be separated by wide intervals, yet."

243. The first words of four lines commonly prefixed to editions of Virgil's *Aeneid*. Modern scholarship judges that the lines were probably not written by Virgil (though they are Virgilian in substance and style) but by a later commentator. See J. W. Mackail's ed. of the *Aeneid* (Oxford: Clarendon Press, 1939), p. 3. The full Latin text runs: "*Ille ego, qui quondam gracili modulatus avena / carmen, et egressus silvis vicina coegi / ut quamvis avido parerent arva colono, / gratum opus agricolis: at nunc horrentia Martis.*" A translation would be as follows: "I am he who once piped his song on the slender reed, and leaving the woods [i.e., the world of pastoral] made the nearby fields give forth their bounty to the tiller of the soil: however great his desire for crops, a work welcome to farmers. But now [I sing] the horrors of Mars." Contrasting the pleasantness of the past with the unpleasantness of the present, the lines look back to the *Georgics* and the *Eclogues* and ahead to the writing of the *Aeneid*, which Virgil began at the request of the Emperor Augustus and always regarded as an unwelcome task. In quoting the "*Ille ego*," Carlyle implies that after the intermezzo of writing the Sterling biography he faced his own "*Aeneid*": what he calls in a later note to Althaus "those 10 years of *Friedrich*"—a labor imposed upon him not by external authority but by his inner sense of duty. He may also imply, given his keen sensitivity to literary allusion, that his own work will attempt epic scope and themes.

244. See *Reminiscences*, II, 200–203, for Carlyle's extended account of his state of mind during the years of *Frederick*, and cf. Sara Norton and M. A. DeWolfe Howe, *Letters of Charles Eliot Norton* (Boston and New York: Houghton Mifflin, 1913), I, 337–338.

described the magnificent struggle to the death against the decadent, hypocritical, amorphous formalism of the *ancien régime* and the unavoidable precondition for the rebirth of a better age. The lectures on "hero-worship," given somewhat later, then developed the other side of the picture: a philosophy of history in which the creative element would triumph over the destructive, and in which all the theoretical and practical qualities of the human mind would be brought together—as in the Pantheon of a new religion—in their most perfect historical manifestations. The work on Cromwell had been intended as the exclusive celebration of one of these heroes, the man who had, in his time, embodied the "urgent need" of the present*: the need for an authoritarian leader. The

* twiddle diddle.

plan to write a history of Frederick the Great was in truth only the picking up again of the same subject but in a later period and on a different foreign soil. A trip to Germany, undertaken in late summer 1852, was the first step in carrying through this plan. With the exception of a quick trip to Paris in 1825, it was the first time that Carlyle had visited the Continent.[245] He went via Rotterdam up the Rhine to Bonn, from there to Frankfurt-am-Main, then to Eisenach, Weimar, Erfurt, Dresden and Berlin. His chief purpose was to study portraits of Frederick's contemporaries; yet the names of the places at which he stayed indicate other purposes as well. For one who ever since his youth had been accustomed to a contemplative,* secluded life, this traveling about was a great nuisance. It

* [*Carlyle changes "beschauliches" (contemplative) to*] "behausliches" [*i.e., home-centered*].

was only to see Goethe's birthplace that he went to Frankfurt, and he made stopovers at Erfurt and Eisenach only to see Luther's cloister, to renew in his rooms in the Wartburg his memories of the heroic age of the Reformation. The visit in Weimar was given over primarily to thinking back over Goethe and Schiller. He tarried the longest—about a week—in Berlin and in those surrounding areas which were, in the best sense, Frederick's own. The whole trip lasted no more than a month: a short time, yet long enough for a traveler who looked at things with so searching and penetrating an eye as Carlyle. Upon his return he made serious

245. Carlyle had made two other trips to the Continent: to the Low Countries in August 1842 and to Paris in October 1851.

preparations to get the work started on this new project. His old house in Chelsea, the same one which he took when he settled down in London two decades earlier, was still, despite the enormous expansion of the capital city, fairly well sheltered from the surrounding roar. Likewise, though for his friends he was at least barely accessible, he never did have many visitors. Moreover, in order that his study might be even more than ever isolated from all external disturbances, he enlarged his house by adding to it a new story whose entire space was occupied by a large room. Here in this attic room he set up his library and study.* All the

* A dreadful enterprise, that proved; such the quack-conditions, quack-workers, the *chaotic* element throughout:—a true *Satan's Invisible World Displayed*;[246] much to the astonishment and frustration of C., who had not enough thought of that, in planning his "*Local*" [*place of business*] or *Saal* [*large room*]!—

books not needed for the history of Frederick were taken out from this library; books which dealt with his subject were acquired in great number, and the further Carlyle progressed the more loaded the bookshelves around him became. It was said of him that he would become like the much-reviled German "Dryasdusts," who when at work envelop themselves and their entire surroundings in smoke and never let their pipes cool off the whole day. But even though he rivaled those "Dryasdusts" in his unremitting diligence, yet the report about the classical cloud of smoke in which he was reputed to work is nonetheless a myth. Carlyle is a smoker, but a moderate one—a smoker of clay pipes. He was accustomed to puff out the curls of little blue clouds in front of him, though less*

* *nimmer* [*never*]; can't do it!—

while at work than in his hours of leisure, stretched out pensively before the fireside or sitting in the garden on a flowervase turned upside down. Moreover, horseback-riding in the parks, or along the banks of the Thames, was his chief recreation.* Sometimes he also took long walks,
* '*Erholung*' quoth-he! I rode some 35,000 miles,—more disgusting to me at last than walking in the Tread-wheel would have been,— during those 10 years of *Friedrich*.

246. "Phrase used in the titles of several books on witchcraft in the seventeenth and eighteenth centuries, notably by Cotton Mather in 1692 and George Sinclair in 1685" (Harrold, *Sartor*, p. 45). On the building of the sound-proof study, see *Reminiscences*, I, 198–200.

of which I will mention only the one most often repeated and surely the most interesting: the walk from Chelsea to the India House in the City,*

* *These* walks had quite *ceased,*—long decades before!

where his friend, the philosopher and economist John Stuart Mill was still employed as an official of the East India Company. Anyone would have been glad to accompany him on this long route through the endless bustle of the big city, and it is pleasant to imagine the meeting of the two men, the two greatest thinkers of present-day England who, each in his own way, have had a greater influence on the development of the political and social, religious and philosophical views of the rising generation in their native land than any other contemporary man-of-letters, Lord Macaulay not excepted.[247] And[248] if one compares the intellectual content of their work with that of the best representatives of the previous generation—Byron, Bentham and Coleridge—it is impossible[249] not to hope for a dramatic turn for the better in the future.*

* [*Carlyle draws a line down the margin from "the two greatest thinkers" to "turn for the better," marks the phrases "two greatest," "Lord Macaulay not excepted," and "turn for the better," and writes in the margin opposite the first:*] Oh, Althaus!

The first two volumes of the *History of Frederick the Great* came out at the end of 1858 and were received with intense public interest, the like of which, among historical works of its time, only Macaulay's *History of England* had ever aroused. As a result, the first edition (as had also happened in Macaulay's case) was sold out as soon as it appeared. As with all of Carlyle's writings, critical judgment was divided between admiration and disparagement. The reader, as always, was deeply impressed by the incomparable vividness of the portrayal, the incisiveness of the characterization, the brilliance of the coloring, the endless profusion of interesting details, the deep pathos, the all-embracing, inexhaustible humor. He still found, however, just as many as ever of the old shortcomings. Indeed, from various sides one heard that the disturbing effect which these created was only aggravated by the huge size of the work, so that the weaknesses in the "Carlylean manner" had just that

247. Althaus (1869) omits "Lord Macaulay not excepted."
248. Althaus (1869) changes to "Afterwards their paths diverged widely; still."
249. Althaus (1869) adds "with all their differences."

much more opportunity to be repeated over and over and thus become fatiguing. Hostile reviewers went so far as to compare the book to the *History of the Adventures of Gargantua and Pantagruel*[250] and to claim that "Rabelais never rioted in greater licence of style, or[251] has more completely set decorum at defiance" as this latest historian of the great Frederick. The general introduction to Prussian history was thought to be too long, overburdened with details, unsatisfactory as a general survey. In the glorification of the brutal Frederick William I, critics saw a strained application of the old Carlylean doctrine of the unity of might and right,*

* Sweet pigsneg [*darling*].

and the superiority of action over words. Especially in this last instance, it was certainly not difficult for them to support their claims by quoting appropriate passages.[252]

A similar mixture of admiration and disparagement came from German reviewers who, as one might expect from the nature of the subject, gave more attention to this work of Carlyle's than they had to all its predecessors. Carlyle, with his numerous idiosyncrasies, struck our German critics as a most interesting eccentric. The mythical characters, Dryasdust and Sauerteig, caused quite a stir, and national pride could hardly accept a favorable judgment of Carlyle after the unceremonious way in which he deemed all the German histories of Frederick the Great to be pathetic and disordered productions of the German Dryasdust, deserving only to be tossed onto the refuse pile of history and forgotten.[253]

*Certainly Carlyle, even in the history of Frederick, must be taken

* n. 1 [*new line*].

exactly as he is, with all his strengths and weaknesses: a powerful, unique personality, and an original, uninhibited intellect, creating and observing according to his own rules and one to whom more than the usual criteria are needed for judgment. Thus he stands, neither seeking friendship nor fearing hostility, a rugged, weather-beaten and powerful Titan who dwells on his rocky heights and against whom the breakers of the sea and the rain and lightning of heaven rage in vain. His is not a logical, analytical

250. Frederick Pollock, in the *Quarterly Review*, 105 (April 1859), 277.
251. Althaus (1869) adds "ever."
252. Althaus (1869) omits "and the superiority . . . passages."
253. Althaus and Carlyle frequently discussed contemporary Prussian historians. See "Erinnerungen," pp. 834, 840–841.

mind but one essentially imaginative and intuitive; he is as much poet and humorist as historian, as much filled with the same universal compassion for the smallest as for the greatest life. At the same time he is a man whose convictions are unshakably rooted in moral principles and to whom it is not enough (as his friend Sterling said of him) "to paint the good which he sees and loves, or see it painted, and enjoy the sight,—not to understand it, and exult in the knowledge of it,—but to take his position upon it, and for it alone to breathe, to move, to fight, to mourn, and die. . . ."[254]

A mind like his, when it turns to the writing of history, cannot, as mentioned before, be measured by conventional standards. He violates from beginning to end the traditional notion of the "dignity of historical writing." He does not give us a polished, stylistically flawless work of art as does Macaulay.* Instead he takes us into his creative workshop

* oh, my friend!—

and permits us to see the scaffolding and materials by means of which he constructs his edifice. And he accompanies the work with comments—as the master would the casting of a bell, as the chorus would the action of a Greek drama, sometimes even as the critical spectator in the pit would the actor's performance on stage. Some of these comments are favorable, some otherwise; some are humorous, some sad. However, they return again and again to the basis of transcendental ideas which his perceptive eye recognizes underlying all apparent change.

*But if the peculiarities of this way of thinking and writing sometimes

* n. 1 [_new line_].

seem pressed to excess and as such can be disturbing, and if its continual variations tire the reader, what other historian whose writing is artistically correct and conforms to the rules can pride himself on such a colorful, vigorous, thoroughly dramatic rendering of a historical period as can Carlyle? Who else can help us to see the events so readily, not only as they arise from their hitherto unrecognized causes but also appear and function as primitive and moral energies? Where else do the characters appear so wonderfully alive on the earth and in the context of their own time? And finally, who so well combines Dryasdust's tireless search for details with Sir Walter Scott's gift for coping with and[255] artistically shaping

254. In the _London and Westminster Review_, 33 (Oct. 1839), 11.
255. Althaus (1869) omits "coping with and."

the chaotic detail into material for historical biography? One may admit that Carlyle went too far* in his condemnation of the "Prussian

* not half way far enough, you mean—not half way so far as the fact!

Dryasdusts," yet his opposition to the pursuit of lifeless scholarship and diligence in the mere assembling of facts is not therefore any the less justified. The unbiased judgment must in the end concede that Carlyle, despite all the peculiarities of his phraseology and of his method of presentation, has produced a work from which even the most knowledge-able authorities on Prussian history and the greatest masters of the art of history can learn. It effectively supports his conviction that historical writing is not a mere repository of facts but the portrayer of human destiny, a cultural teacher of the human spirit.

[*After this paragraph Carlyle inserts in brackets the following sentence*:] Alas, my Althaus, you too know almost nothing about it!

The work had originally been estimated at four volumes; but when the first two volumes reached no further than the point of the death of Frederick William I a further expansion was easily predictable. After he completed the first two volumes in the autumn of 1858, Carlyle undertook a second trip to Germany to study Frederick the Great's battlefields. This trip lasted six weeks and its results are readily apparent in the parts of the *History* which followed. A strictly military evaluation of Carlyle's accounts of operations and his battle descriptions must be left to the military expert. If, however, insofar as the purpose is to give the reader a clear understanding of the operations and a view of the course of the fighting, then Carlyle's narrative could not be improved upon. He unfolds before us the course of the military events with the same incomparable vividness with which he describes the social and political ferment of the eighteenth century.[256] The same dramatic interest, the same feeling for the local situation, transports us back to the battlefields of the Silesian and Seven Years' Wars, into the castles of the kings, the salons of high society, and the council meetings of ministers and generals. And above the tumult of events and the great masses of toiling and suffering humanity there hovers the figure of the great king—clear, impressionable, full of

256. See Thomas Carlyle, *Journey to Germany Autumn 1858*, ed. R. A. E. Brooks (New Haven: Yale University Press, 1940), pp. xxiii–xxiv.

character, in vital immediate presence, and who as ruler looks after the fate of his kingdom, surmounts all obstacles placed by destiny, and emerges victorious from the struggle against the world in arms. From the abundance of interesting incidents let us simply consider that which has to do with Frederick's relationship with Voltaire, which in all its historical ramifications and involvements was probably never before depicted so fully and with such an inexhaustible wealth of characteristic details. And if in a six-volume work of about 4,000 pages there are occasional passages which the reader is tempted to read over more quickly than others, and assertions and explanations which are based upon false premises, this is, after all, hardly surprising. Even if un-challenged as to knowledge of human relationships or unstimulated in thinking and feelings, no one can neglect the reading of such passages and, once having come to the end of the last volume, he will be forced to admit that he has experienced the outpouring of a mind to whose teach-ings, paradoxical as they may seem at times, he will often return again in the hope of learning more.

The last volume of the *History of Frederick the Great* came out near the end* of last year (1865). It remains only for us to cast a final glance

* '*end*' of 1864 or nearly so.

at two events which have taken place in Carlyle's life since then. English critics have congratulated him on at last reaching the end of such a long project and one (it was hinted) in which his initial enthusiasm* for the

* alas, never had any;—only some *enthusiasmus* for the teachings that might lie in such a *Gegenstand* [*subject*], and for working (honestly) while it was called to-day; in neither of which respects did said '*enthusiasmus*' much abate, in spite of all the discourage-ments there were.— — Althaus is not worth reading any farther than to this point; and the reading of the rest would perhaps give me pain again. I will stop for today, possibly for altogether, and tie him up out of the way (Chelsea, September 8*th*, 1866;—been considerably *interrupted* by "Eyre Defence Committee"[257] &c &c).

subject had cooled. It was thought that once relieved of the burden of pursuing this foreign subject he would now be able to concentrate his

257. Formed in August 1866 to provide funds for the defence of Edward John Eyre, Governor of Jamaica. Its first meeting, which Carlyle attended, was on 29 August.

inexhaustible energy more directly to working on subjects that were both more familiar and closer to home. *Whether and in what way this

*(Have read no farther at present (10 September 1866) [)].

assumption will be realized remains to be seen. At present, the historian of Frederick the Great is still resting on his recent laurels,[258] and no one has heard that he intends to take on a new labor.

Of the two events mentioned the first was a proud and happy one. The students of the University of Edinburgh have the right each year to elect their Lord Rector, and for the year 1865–1866 they chose to honor in this way their great countryman Thomas Carlyle. According to custom, at each election two candidates are put up representing the two inevitable parties, the Whigs and the Tories, the Liberals and the Conservatives, which separate university students just as they do all the other classes of society in England. In this same way, Carlyle had already been proposed as a candidate for the office of Lord Rector a number of years ago, first in Aberdeen, then in Glasgow. These nominations are the responsibility solely of the students, and the charge that the candidates themselves actually apply (as the continental newspapers occasionally say) is false. In Aberdeen and Glasgow, Carlyle's supporters had remained a minority; in Edinburgh, at the last election for Rector, he won by a respectable majority of the votes over his rival Disraeli. Even now he hesitated for a long time whether he should accept that office and that distinction—he who throughout his entire life had never sought an office or distinction[259] other than such as his natural talents imposed upon him: to be the teacher of his age and of his people. At last he gave his consent. This spontaneous homage by the youth of Scotland, the third generation which had risen to maturity since his own student years in Edinburgh, meant much to him, as he acknowledged in his inaugural address, because it was "a touching and tragic, and yet at the same time beautiful" recognition that he had not toiled in this world altogether in vain.[260] He promised the customary inaugural address for the beginning of the spring, and on 2 April 1866 his service in this office began. People had already

258. Althaus (1869) adds "and with the exception of a new 'Latter-Day Pamphlet,' that which under the unusual title *Shooting Niagara* opposed the Reform Bill of 1867, neither has a new work flowed from his pen."

259. In the late 1820's and early 1830's Carlyle had sought professorships in several of the Scottish universities and in the new University of London.

260. Quoted and paraphrased from *Works*, XXIX, 449.

been looking forward to this event for a long time and with intense expectation, and from all parts of England and Scotland Carlyle's friends and admirers hastened to the Scottish Athens to hear and possibly to see him. The great Music Hall of the city, the most spacious public building in Edinburgh, proved far too small for the crowds pressing to get in, so that only a relatively small number of the out-of-town visitors accomplished the purpose of their trip. Nothing need be said of the enthusiastic reception accorded the Lord Rector[261] and of the impression which his extemporaneous hour-and-a-half speech made, for both are of very recent memory.[262] Suffice it to say that his speech presented once again a true picture of his well-known philosophy of life, and that its meaning had application for him not only as the speaker but also as an author and as a man, as the hero of *Sartor Resartus*, as the historian of Cromwell and of the French Revolution, and finally as the stoic scholar who with his powerful personality represented to a rare degree of perfection the highest universal goal of all men: the unity of life and thought. One more characteristic incident deserves notice. At the inaugural ceremony a number of famous men were to be awarded honorary doctorates, and Carlyle himself had been proposed as one to be honored. But he declined in a letter which said in effect that he had a brother who was a doctor, and in the event that two Dr. Carlyles were to appear in Paradise* unpleasant

* pig! This is Newspaper nonsense, *in toto* or nearly so.

misunderstandings might result. For this and other reasons he preferred, for his part, to remain Mr. Thomas Carlyle. And with this decision the matter was closed.

The second of the events mentioned above was a sorrowful one. Nineteen days after his address as Rector in Edinburgh, on 21 April, while Carlyle was still away in Scotland, his faithful wife, whose noble sympathy had so long brightened and adorned his lonely life, died suddenly. From all that one hears, she was a woman of most rare qualities of mind and heart, a woman to whom one can well apply Carlyle's own words when he mourned the death of the wife of his friend John Sterling: "his other self, who had faithfully attended him so long in all his pilgrimings, cheerily footing the heavy tortuous ways along with him, can

261. Changed in Althaus (1869) to "The reception accorded the Lord Rector was enthusiastic."
262. "For ... memory" omitted in Althaus (1869).

follow him no farther; sinks now at his side: 'The rest of your pilgrimings alone, O Friend,—adieu, adieu!' She too is forever hidden from his eyes; and he stands, on the sudden, very solitary amid the tumult of fallen and falling things."[263] In Mrs. Carlyle's case death came so suddenly that Carlyle had no* reason to come** back to his now wholly desolate home[265]

* doppelt [double].
** eilen [hurry].[264]

in Chelsea. The body was taken to Scotland and probably* in accordance

*[Carlyle crosses out "probably"].

with a decision already* made earlier was buried in the family vault of

*[Carlyle inserts "lang," crosses it out and substitutes] längst [a long time].[266]

Dr. Welsh in Haddington.

For the "solitary" remainder of Carlyle's "pilgrimings" let us express only one hope: that he may be allowed to bear the burden of this last sorrow, as of the many others, with unbowed strength. In full awareness of his completed life's work and in retrospect over the germination of the seeds his mind planted, may it be granted to him to feel the powerful effect of that "marching-music of humanity"[267] of Goethe's poem with which he closed his Edinburgh address—right to the clarion call "We bid you be of hope."[268]

I did "read no farther" than the place in p. 40[p. 119]; nor looked at any thing,—except where the previous pencil marks (end of p. 41 [p. 120], opposite) led me to the slight marginalia there. I now tie up this poor Article; put it away, amongst things of Hers; and shall, very possibly never see it again,—except outside of it, when on its road to the fire.— — If I don't burn it, those that come after me are again charged to be cautious; & to consider well, in

263. Works, XI, 247.
264. Cf. Reminiscences, I, 249–253.
265. Althaus (1869) omits "now wholly."
266. According to Reminiscences, I, 254, a "covenant of forty years back," i.e., made at the time of their marriage.
267. Works, XXIX, 481.
268. Ibid., p. 482. Carlyle never tired of repeating with reverence the last line of Goethe's poem "Symbolum."

this case and in all others, *what* it will be useful to print, for such a public as ours, and what to withhold, of these jottings about *Her* or about myself. Endless *silence* about us both,—that really would be my wish (*more* 'really,' in my present now habitual mood, than anybody thinks); but that is probably impossible or unattainable: and instead of hazy nonsense throughout, here and there a bit of certainty may have its advantages,—if they can be had cheap. Adieu, O Survivor; study to walk wisely till thou join me.

T. Carlyle

(Chelsea, Monday 10 September 1866).

REMINISCENCE OF
ADAM AND ARCHIBALD SKIRVING

Editor's Introduction

Carlyle's account of the farmer Adam Skirving and his son Archibald extends the passing mention in the *Reminiscences*. Reading Adam Skirving's ballad "Tranent Muir" again in David Herd's *Collection of Scots Songs* (1776) seems to have prompted Carlyle to write about the Skirvings. The ballad tells of a Lieutenant Peter Smith's cowardice at the Battle of Prestonpans, in which Charles Edward's Highlanders routed the English forces under Sir John Cope in September 1745. After recounting an incident in which the canny Adam Skirving humorously deflates a friend of the lieutenant's sent to offer him a challenge, Carlyle moves on by natural association to draw an unforgettable pen portrait of his son, the temperamental Archibald, whose life crossed for a while the young Jane Welsh's and, briefly, his own.

Adam Skirving (1719–1803) was a prosperous farmer who lived at Garleton, near Haddington. His father had farmed Prestonmains, very close to the site of the Battle of Prestonpans. Adam was educated at Prestonkirk and, if never a scholar, read widely during his lifetime in history, geography, and astronomy. He was also an indefatigable sportsman, fond of horses, hounds, curling, and especially golf. Although he took no part in the Rebellion of 1745, he did compose the ballads "Hey Johnnie Cope," included in Hogg's *Jacobite Relics*, and "Tranent Muir." He was famed for his verbal repartee but disliked the task of writing. By his two marriages he had three sons: Archibald, an artist; Robert, a soldier; and David, a farmer.[1]

Archibald Skirving (1749–1819) became a painter and miniaturist of

---

1. On the Skirvings, see James Johnson and William Stenhouse, *The Scots Musical Museum* (Edinburgh and London: William Blackwood and Sons, 1853), IV, *189–198*; and, especially, B. C. Skinner, "Archibald Skirving and His Work," *Transactions of the East Lothian Antiquarian and Field Naturalists' Society*, 12 (1970), 46–56. Skinner's article includes a list of Skirving's portraits of which the identity of the sitter is known.

note in Edinburgh. When he was about twenty-eight, he gave up his clerkship in the Customs Office to devote himself wholly to portraiture. He studied first in London, returned to Edinburgh, then in 1786 went to Rome, where he spent most of the next eight years. On his return voyage he was captured (4 August 1794) by the French, imprisoned in Brest as a spy, and did not get to Scotland until August 1795—his vision impaired and his personality affected by his prison experience. Settling in Edinburgh, he worked mainly in pastel and crayon. He could command one hundred guineas for a head in pastel, more than many established artists could get for a portrait in oils. Scott speaks of him, in a letter to Samuel Rogers of 30 May 1816, as "an unrivalled artist as a painter in crayons."[2] The National Gallery of Scotland and the Scottish National Portrait Gallery hold examples of his work. He wrote at least one poem, painted a well-known portrait of Burns, another of Grace Welsh (Jane Welsh Carlyle's mother), and two of his father.

Of the other two sons of Adam Skirving, we know less. Robert Skirving (post 1749–post 1838) survived his elder brother by at least nineteen years and may have been considerably younger than he was. He joined the army of the East India Company, rising to the rank of captain, and served in the East Indies until 1806, when he returned to Scotland and settled at Croys, a farm two miles north of Castle Douglas in Kirkcudbrightshire. He inherited something of his father's poetic talent. Of David, Adam's son by his second marriage, we know only that he was a farmer and friendly with the Welsh family.

Carlyle wrote his sketch of the Skirvings on 17 January 1868, in the depths of a bleak London winter. He was evidently still depressed by the death of his wife, nearly two years before, and felt helpless before the memories of the past which swirled about him. A letter he wrote on 23 January to his old friend Thomas Erskine voices the mood which suffuses the sketch: "I am very idle here, very solitary, which I find to be oftenest less miserable to me than the common society that offers. It is a great evil to me that now I have no work, none worth calling by that name; that I am too weak, too languid, too sad of heart, to be fit for any work, in fact to care sufficiently for any object left me in the world, to think of grappling round it and coercing it by work. . . . *Basta basta*, I for most part say of it,

2. *The Letters of Sir Walter Scott*, ed. H. J. C. Grierson and others, 12 vols. (London: Constable & Co., 1933), IV, 243.

and look with longings towards the still country where at last we and our loved ones shall be together again. Amen, amen!"[3]

The multitudinous writings by or on the Carlyles have not yielded other significant references to the Skirvings mentioned in this reminiscence. David G. Ritchie published a letter from Jane Welsh Carlyle to Robert Scot Skirving and one to his aunt, Mary Scot, her schoolfriend, in his *Early Letters of Jane Welsh Carlyle*. Robert Scot Skirving (1821–1900), whose father was David Skirving, corresponded with Ritchie in 1889. (The correspondence is preserved in the Edinburgh University Library.) It resulted in Ritchie including in his book Skirving's recollections of the spring day, probably in 1834, when he saw Jane Welsh Carlyle sit silently for a full half-hour bent over her father's tomb. In a letter to Ritchie of 2 April 1889 he describes himself as "an East Lothian man & my Father & Mother were both very intimate with the Welshes." At Mrs. Carlyle's request he visited the Carlyles at Cheyne Row in 1847, entered however into an argument with Carlyle, and did not see him again until 1866, when he served as a pallbearer at Mrs. Carlyle's funeral.

Carlyle always valued the gift of painting in words. "A man with pen in his hand," he wrote Varnhagen von Ense in 1845, "with the gift of articulate pictural utterance, surely *he* is well employed in painting and articulating worthy acts and men that by the nature of them were dumb. I on the whole define all Writing to mean even that, or else almost nothing."[4] He prized in Archibald Skirving two of the character traits that he prized in himself: rugged independence in all personal dealings and scorn for the world's opinion. He did not, however, carry his insistence on independence to the extreme that Skirving did. As he seizes the intense individuality and craggy manhood of this singular human being, we see Carlyle's "gift of articulate pictural utterance" to superb effect.

The manuscript of the Skirving reminiscence, also in Carlyle's later hand, is catalogued in the National Library of Scotland under the number 1798 (ix). With it is a fair copy made at Carlyle's request by Madame Emilie Venturi, a friend who occasionally served as amanuensis. Rather

3. Richard Herne Shepherd, *Memoirs of the Life and Writings of Thomas Carlyle* . . . (London: W. H. Allen, 1881), II, 256–257.
4. *The Last Words of Thomas Carlyle* (New York: Appleton, 1892), p. 304.

than attempt to record the many variants, I follow the manuscript in Carlyle's hand but incorporate in my text his revisions of Madame Venturi's fair copy, on the assumption that these revisions represent his final thoughts.

From "TRANENT MUIR" (i.e. *Battle of Prestonpans*),
by Skirving, A Farmer near Haddington (in 1745)

> But Gard'ner brave did still behave
>   Like to a hero bright man [. . . .]
> While he had breath to draw, man.
>
> And Major Bowle, that worthy soul,
>   Was brought down to the ground, man;
> His horse being shot, it was his lot
>   There for to get many a wound, man:
>
> Lieutenant Smith, of Irish birth,
>   Frae whom he call'd for aid, man,
> Being full of dread, lap o'er his head,
>   And wadna be gainsaid, man.
>
> He made sic haste, sae spurr'd his beast,
>   'Twas little there he saw, man;
> To Berwick rade, there safely said
>   The Scots were rebels a' man:
> But let that end, for weel 'tis kenn'd
>   His use and wont's to lie, man:
> The Teague is naught, he never faught
>   When he had room to flee, man

[from *Herd's* Collection of *Scots Songs*
(Edinburgh 1776) i.iii][1]

By these rough stanzas on Smith there still hangs a tale, in Skirving's native region,[2] where the fame of him ruggedly lives.

Smith[3] was a Lieutenant of *Horse* (seemingly), used to

---

1. Carlyle's brackets. His transcription shows unimportant variants from published texts.

2. East Lothian, or Haddingtonshire.

3. Lieutenant Peter Smith remains little more than the outline of a personality. He was, according to Skirving's ballad, of Irish blood, and his regiment of dragoons,

Haddington Barracks, and familiar in society there. Returning after the Rebellion was over, he found this Ballad in everybody's mouth, and the Two Stanzas inconveniently twinkling up on him, wherever he shew'd face. After painful meditation he resolved on calling out Farmer Skirving (no hope of making him *recant* by milder methods, what he knew to be a fact); and sent a military Friend with his challenge, written or oral, I now forget *which*. The military Friend found Skirving in his Farm-Yard ("Girlton,"[4] Garwald-town?—that was still his *Son's* Farm in my time), busy, with his men round him, "filling dung," i.e. forking it into carts for the ploughing field. Skirving paused, struck-down his "graip" (big three-pronged fork) and, resting his hands on the same ('one of the best-natured, and most athletic of men,' says his Tombstone, to this day),[5]—listened attentively to Smith's Messenger. Deliberately heard, &, where necessary, questioned him, till the affair became quite clear;—whereupon, affair being clear in all points, Skirving, still leaning on his graip, made the following memorable answer: "God, I never saw Lieutenant Smith, I dinna ken whether I can fecht [*fight*] him or not: but if he come up here, I'll tak a look o' him; and if I think I can fecht him, I will; if not, I'll rin awa' as he did!"—and immediately resumed his forking, perhaps

---

commanded by a Colonel Hamilton, was stationed at Haddington in 1745. Major Richard Bowles, whom Smith was supposed to have deserted on the field of battle, also served in this regiment at Prestonpans. It is not clear that Smith actually fled the field over the wounded Major's body, nor that he was a coward. When the enlisted men saw the Highlanders charging with their claymores, they broke ranks and nothing the officers could do stopped them. According to the official report, the officers without exception did all they could to rally their men before themselves fleeing. If this report is correct, as seems likely, Smith had good reason to be angry at Skirving. He tried to clear his name without resorting to a challenge. Major Bowles published a denial of Smith's cowardice in the *Edinburgh Courant* of 6 January 1746, and denied as well that Smith had refused to help him when he was wounded. When the article was ignored, Smith felt compelled to offer the challenge—which led to Carlyle's story.

4. "Girlton," actually Garleton, was a farm two miles north of Haddington on the Gosford road. Adam Skirving was tenant there in 1745 and upon his death the farm was taken over by his son David.

5. The complete inscription is given in Johnson and Stenhouse, *The Scots Musical Museum* (Edinburgh and London: William Blackwood and Sons, 1853), IV, 197*. It reads in part, "One of the most Athletic and Best Tempered of Men," but refers not to Adam but to his father Archibald Skirving, who farmed Muirton and "lived only 56 years." Cf. *Reminiscences*, II, 86.

with new diligence for this *Smith* parenthesis, which had interrupted his men and him. Cartel Smith is no more heard of in
history.[6]

This story I believe to be perfectly true; otherwise I should not
think of writing it down, least of all *now*. Various other Anecdotes,
of the same rugged homely stamp, are current of Skirving; who,
and whose people, were frequently a topic at this hearth, in better
days long past. The first time I went to Haddington, 46 years ago,[7]
on a summer afternoon, on foot with Edward Irving, day ever-
memorable to me, I well recollect our climbing the wall of Athelstaneford ("*Elshinford*") Churchyard,[8] and reading the above-
mentioned bit of Inscription on Skirving's Tombstone: tho' Home
(of *Douglas* Tragedy),[9] once Minister of that Parish of "Elshinford," had probably been our main errand there. I still seem to *see*
this Skirving memorial-stone (near by the corner of the wall where
we got over); a sound upright slab of sandstone, biggish, & the
entire Inscription rather long, letters all sharp as if new, tho' the
coat of lichens was evident; and have entirely forgotten Home and
the birthplace of *Douglas*, having, I suppose, next to no interest
whatever in him or it.

Two Sons of Skirving by his first marriage, notable men both, I
have seen; and the younger of them,[10] an Ex-Captain of Foot, who
lived and whose son lives at Croys in Galloway, some 12 miles
from Craigenputtoch, I slightly knew. By a second marriage there
was another son[11] (Farmer at "Girlton," as I suppose *his* son still
is), whose Daughter had been a schoolmate of *One* who always
held her schoolmates in warm regard, and delighted to speak of
her school-days!— Some controversy about heritage had risen
between the two Skirving families; and they lived silently es-
tranged from one another. Proud enough all, I suppose; especially

6. In his story "Cruthers and Jonson: or, The Outskirts of Life," written in 1822,
Carlyle had dealt with the Battle of Prestonpans in an ironic way. See *Works*, XXX,
180–182.

7. In late May 1821.

8. Athelstaneford ("*Elshinford*" indicates the pronunciation) is a village seventeen
miles east of Edinburgh and four miles north of Haddington.

9. John Home (1722–1808) was the author of the once popular romantic tragedy
Douglas, based on a Scottish ballad and first acted in 1756.

10. Captain Robert Skirving.

11. David Skirving.

those two sons of family first, who were known as men of equity, veracity, and generosity, but of inflexible self-will; and were held in a higher than common regard, their half-brother standing only in a highish tho' common,—never of much note to *Her* or Hers, as I could gather.

The elder of these two Brothers, *Ballad* Skirving's eldest Son, was, in my time, a Painter in Edinburgh, said to be of consummate skill in Portraiture, but living in a secluded, almost *mythic* condition; refusing all work except upon his own whims; and carelessly said by the public to be "cracked" in brain. Which indeed, I suppose, he almost was. In his young days he had gone to Italy enthusiastic for Art-Culture; had fallen among Napoleon's soldierings, been seized as a spy, narrowly missed being shot at once; had then lain long in damp dungeons, in constant danger of his life; and, before deliverance could come, had got his nerves incurably exasperated; a condition which the contradictions of the world, on his return, especially which the shortcomings and obliquities of mankind, inexpressibly detestable to Skirving, had made worse instead of better, and fixed into permanency in the indignant man. Of his skill in painting I can myself speak. His Brother at Croys once, with much mystery and emotion, took me to a very private repository in the House, and opening various locks, and at last a casket within them all, graciously shewed me a Miniature of his late Father, by his Brother now also gone (both of whom he seemed to venerate with proud piety); by far the best Portrait I had then ever seen of any man;[12] and which I vividly remembered again, 10 years after, on sight of the first real *Oliver Cromwell* by *Cooper*,—real, not fictitious & imaginary, as above nine-tenths of them are,—which was vouchsafed me.[13] Nothing so excellent had I ever seen before.

12. This was an oval miniature on china, approximately 2″ × 1½″, which is now owned by Mrs. Leila Hoskins, Cheltenham, England. Unfortunately it was so badly damaged in transit from Edinburgh to Cheltenham in 1944 that its reproduction here would give it the effect of a caricature. Therefore, I have included another painting of his father by Archibald, an oil 29½″ × 24½″, then owned by David Skirving, now by the Scottish National Portrait Gallery. It is related in design to the miniature.

13. Carlyle saw the portrait of Cromwell—an 11″ × 14″ in crayon—on the evening of 8 September 1842 hanging in the hall of Sidney Sussex College, Cambridge, ten years and one month after he saw the miniature of Adam Skirving while visiting

Skirving would, *impromptu* now & then, do admirable Likenesses, with a burnt stick or bit of chalk, on the board of a pair of bellows; but as to sitters, he had his inexorable whims; and many faces there were which no reward or penalty would so much as induce him to try: "No, no; can't be done!" —"And why, then?" He declined to tell why; no use pressing him to say why. One positive Lady, pressing him over much, got this: "The real reason, Madam is, I don't want to raise the price of yellow-ochre!" Sitters whom he did accept had to know that it was on strict terms and only as a favour. Lady Charlotte Campbell, famed beauty of Edinburgh and of the world, Duke of Argyll's Sister,[14] and at that time in her meridian height, had got him persuaded; dress, headdress and details were all accurately settled, and the first sitting went off altogether well. At the second sitting, something in the headdress had been altered, Beauty, on second thoughts, discovering some improvement possible there. Skirving flew angry; remonstrated with emphasis, "Can't stand the like of this, Madam!"—was, however, flattered and persuaded into standing it; and again made a successful and hopeful stage, or sitting. Capricious Beauty, I suppose, was herself flattered at subduing & seducing the fiery creature; and tried it a second time; came for her third sitting, in headdress again slightly altered: but this time, Skirving threw down his brush; inexorable to apologies, persuasions, and entreaties; and no third sitting was or ever could be.

As is easy to fancy, Sitters on these terms altogether disappeared; and fiery Skirving was left more and more to his solitudes and silent reflexions & indignations. For perhaps the last 20 or 15 years of his life, he lived in some *Flat* or Lodging all his own (I think, in what was called "The Terrace," at the head of Leith

---

Capt. Robert Skirving on the morning of 13 August 1832. According to David Piper, "the attribution of the Sidney Sussex drawing to [Samuel] Cooper is no longer generally accepted; it is related in detail to the Lily [or Lely] paintings rather than the Cooper miniatures, and is doubtless an early copy of one of the former" (*Catalogue of Seventeenth-Century Portraits in the National Portrait Gallery 1625–1714* [Cambridge: Cambridge University Press, 1963]). Early editions of Carlyle's *Cromwell* as well as that in the Centenary *Works* carry as frontispiece Francis Holl's engraving of another of these copies of one of the paintings by Sir Peter Lely (1618–1680).

14. (1775–1861), sister to George William Campbell, 6th Duke of Argyll (1768–1839). The portrait of Lady Charlotte survives unfinished in Mrs. Hoskins's collection.

Walk), in complete Hermitage; an indignant but uncomplaining King, supreme sovereign there if nowhere else. He had some peculium of funds which sufficed him; by temperance and exercise he kept himself in perfect health. Some few, the chosen of the world, he warmly loved; to the multitudinous vulgar, titled and untitled, rich or not rich, he had long since waved his stern *apage* [*be gone*], and was not concerned with them farther. In the fine times of year he went roving a good deal on miscellaneous sudden visits & excursions to his favourites, oftenest in native East-Lothian. For bad weather, I suppose he had some few select Books; and certainly he had a *Lathe*, and did much turning. On sight of a fine "*beef-bone*" (thigh-bone in a "round of beef") in a friend's house, he would politely beg the Lady to save it for him; and would, by and by, work it into something (*egg-cups* oftenest) as a salutation gift in some other of his favourite houses. He usually appeared quite on the sudden: "In our house," said my Darling, "it was frequently at breakfast time; he would have in his hand, now and then, some small neat gift, a tiny basket with 4 or 5 fresh eggs (or the like, if they were scarce); something of his own handiwork, bit of turning from his lathe, was the most distinguished gift of all. He was well-liked and esteemed among us; and flowed out into cheerful and curious talk whenever he sat down."— There are *two* of his *bone egg-cups* still in this house; which were relieved from service here, by my direction, 8 or 9 years ago, and reposited in some safe place, in honour of the wayward man of genius,—should anybody ever prize them for his sake or ours! They were excellent for their use; stood firm on their base (hourglass shape, and *base* or head could alternate); kept your eggs *warm* as no crockery or metal will; and had long been favourites with me, when I made the effort & dismissed them, knowing well enough I should not see their equal again!—

Dr Welsh and Household (which I can't wonder at) seem to have been especially distinguished in the mind of Skirving. Veracity of head and of heart, intellect practical, speculative; valour, pity, native nobleness of mind and manners: all this was the wild man's passion; all this, conjoined with recognition, sympathy and tolerant kindness to the wild man's self, must have made the scene welcome enough, and much the element for him. I know not when he first grew to come familiarly;—perhaps about *her* 6th or 7th year?[15] He might well love and admire the bright ingenuous little Child; and delight to have her fluttering about him, and perching trustfully like a Bird of Paradise upon his wild tusks! His talk generally, even to her, was of rugged sincerity, oftenest with a dash of satire; but it was evident he liked her better and better.

When it came to school-years, & she had to go to Edinburgh for her teaching, he openly expressed his encouragements, his determination to help her himself, with his best art, in the matter of Drawing, at least. She went accordingly to his grim Hermitage several times; found the cheerfullest welcome; the place very dusty, littery, idle-looking; and the man intent rather on talking to her, than on teaching with any diligence or clear method. Strange art-precepts he did give her here and there; which she could not then understand. The tasks he set her were impractical, his criticisms were rigorously severe. He liked far best to carry her about to the chosen Edinburgh friends he had, and shew her off, set her talking &c;—which she herself, tho' then but fourteen or so, and living at old Cousin Bradfute's (I suppose),[16] under her own control, disliked, found to be unsuitable, mainly a waste of time in regard to Drawing; and soon altogether gave up; I rather think not without some transitory indignation on the part of Skirving. Who however, on reflecting, would not fail to approve. An ample fine mahogany Drawing-board, a gift of his, stood long among our House-hold goods unused:—and indeed still stands,[17] where no one but myself would suspect it,—not now useless, but thriftily (with a noble *thrift*, and *reality* of "talent," which I prize far beyond Three-volume Novels, or California nuggets) changed into the main part of a *Table* in the spare-room here!— This wild man and his exaggerations and perverse violences is strangely gilded over to my mind, and made memorable and interesting by a light not his. He was unwise, could gain no victory in this world; and is

---

15. 1807 or 1808.

16. John Bradfute (1764–1837), bookseller and uncle to Jane Welsh's good friend Eliza Stodart. In 1807 he moved to 22 George Square, where Miss Welsh stayed during her visits to Edinburgh.

17. Neither the drawing-board nor the bone egg-cups are listed in the most recent catalog of the Carlyle House in Chelsea.

now in himself Nothing or not much. But he is part of the sacred
VANISHED LAND; the sacredest of all, and the beautifully saddest,
now that there remains for one no PROMISED LAND any more!—

I once saw this Skirving, once only: in Edinburgh,—must have
been 1818 or '19, more probably the former.[18] Edward Irving and I
must have crossed from Fife very early, in a summer morning;—
I have quite forgotten about that, and it is all dark and abolished
for me: but what I vividly remember is that we were swiftly
stepping southward, along South-Bridge Street, when just at the
utmost corner of it, on the east side,—I think, out of the street
disjoining it from Nicholson Street,—there stept swiftly upon us
an aged promenading gentleman, of notable appearance, whom
Irving, fixing my attention by some whisper "This is Skirving,"
cordially accosted, with the ordinary salutations, getting response
which was also cordial or kind, but had less of joy or eagerness in
the manner of it. I said nothing, but watched, and have a "Picture"
of it still which Skirving himself could not beat. The morning was
balmy and beautiful, with a soft breeze blowing everywhere, sky
as bright as diamonds, bright sunshine, but none of it yet reaching
us in our street-path (opposite the s.e. corner of the College),
street still rather empty: one of the finest possible mornings for a
long promenade, which I suppose Skirving had been upon, over in
the Arthur-Seat region, and was returning. An altogether striking
man. Wiry, elastic, perpendicular, and of good inches, still brisk-
looking, tho' perhaps 70 odd; spotlessly clean, his linen white as
snow, no necktie but a loosish-fastened black ribbon; hair all grey,
not white, nor over-long; face, neck, hands of a fine brown tint;
one of the cleanest old men I ever saw;—and such a face as you
would still more rarely see. Eagle-like; nose hooked like an eagle's
bill, eyes still with something of the eagle's flash in them; squarish
prominent brow, under-jaw ditto, cheeks & neck thin, sensitively
wrinkled,—brow, cheek, jaws, chin all betokening impetuosity,
rapidity, delicacy, and the stormy fire of genius not yet hidden
under the ashes of old age. A face and figure never to be forgotten.
His brother of Croys has something of the same physiognomy,

18. The most likely date is the summer of 1818, since Carlyle left Kirkcaldy to live
in Edinburgh in the autumn of 1818.

less developed. His Father's, to judge[19] by the Portrait, must have been very different: a face full of rustic sagacity, humour and character, that too, but massive in type, broad-oval, thoroughly eupaptic, and with nothing of aquiline in it.

Painter Skirving went on his way, and I saw him no more. My Jeannie I had not yet seen, or much ventured to hope seeing. She would be at Haddington that morning! Her Father still flourishing, nobly busy; and sorrow and its bitterness unknown to her. O thou strange VANISHED LAND!

(Jan. 17*th* 1868)

---

19. The manuscript in Carlyle's hand ends here. For the remainder of the reminiscence I have followed Madame Venturi's fair copy.

Thomas Carlyle, about 1867: photograph by Julia Margaret Cameron. *Courtesy of the Metropolitan Museum of Art, The Alfred Stieglitz Collection, New York.*

elften Jahre (1806) auf das Gymnasium (Grammar School) in die benachbarte kleine Stadt Annan. Wie es ihm dort erging, findet sich unschwer erkennbar im „Sartor Resartus" angedeutet. „Ich war ein Fremder unter Fremden", läßt er Professor Teufelsdröckh von sich sagen. Das wilde rohe Wesen der Schulkameraden mißfiel ihm; er hielt sich von ihren Spielen fern, weinte viel, ja so viel, daß er den Beinamen „der Weinende" empfing, der auch (so gesteht er) bis zu seinem 13. Jahre nicht ganz unverdient war. „Meine Lehrer", heißt es an einer andern Stelle, „waren schweinslederne Pedanten, ohne Kenntniß der menschlichen oder der Knabennatur. Sie stopften uns voll mit zahllosen todten Wörtern, und nannten das Pflege des Geistes. Griechisch und lateinisch wurde mechanisch gelehrt, hebräisch kaum einmal das, vieles andere, was sie Geschichte, Kosmographie, Philosophie und so fort nannten, so gut wie gar nicht", sodaß, wäre er selbst nicht seiner Gewohnheit gemäß in den Werkstätten der Handwerker umhergewandert, wo er viele Dinge lernte, und hätte er sich nicht außerdem fleißig mit Privatlektüre beschäftigt, seiner Meinung nach seine Zeit völlig würde verschwendet gewesen sein. Wer erkennt in diesen Zügen nicht schon das Vorbild der sensitiven Natur, des ernsten, unbefriedigten, idealistischen, resignirten „weinenden Philosophen" späterer Jahre? Doch wenn sein unbefriedigtes Gemüth von der Routine des Schulwesens zu selbstgewählter Arbeit und zu den Werkstätten des praktischen Lebens seine Zuflucht nahm, so kam trotzdem das positive Wissen der Schule nicht bei ihm zu kurz. Sein Gedächtniß war ebenso vortrefflich als sein Fleiß und seine Lernfähigkeit groß, und da die Gabe, eine Fülle bunter Details zu bewältigen, ihm nicht minder eigen war, als der Hang zu idealistischem Denken, so bewältigte er auch den spröden Stoff des Schulwissens und wurde bereits nach drei Jahren von dem Gymnasium in Annan auf die Universität Edinburgh entlassen (1809).

Seine Aeltern hatten ihn, wie gesagt, für eine theologische Carriere bestimmt. Aber in den schottischen und englischen Hochschulen sind die Facultäten weniger streng geschieden als in Deutschland, und auch für den Studiosus theologiae galten die althergebrachten Branchen der Classiker und der Mathematik (Classics and Mathematics) zunächst als Hauptgegenstände des Studiums. Näheres von Carlyle's classischen Studien hören wir nicht; auch sucht man vergebens in seiner ganzen spätern Entwickelung nach einem geistigen Reflex des antiken Lebens, der antiken Literatur. Es scheint, als habe jene Welt von Anfang an seinen Interessen fern gelegen, oder doch seine Sympathien nicht entzündet. Vielleicht stieß schon in seiner Jugend ihn naiv egoistisches, leichtlebiges Wesen ihn ab. Ohne Frage übten die spätern Geschichtsepochen des Mittelalters, der Reformation und der Revolution stets einen tiefern Einfluß auf ein Gemüth aus, das den Bruch zwischen Natur und Geist mit erschütternder Gewalt im Innersten fühlte und mit leidenschaftlicher Energie nach einer Versöhnung der streitenden Elemente, nach einer praktischen Richtschnur in dem bunten Wirrwarr der Welt rang, in welche das Schicksal ihn hingestellt hatte. Die Mathematik betrieb er dagegen mit großem Eifer und ebenso eifrig nahm er an den philosophischen Discussionen theil, welche damals unter Dugald Stewart's Vorsitz in Edinburgh geführt wurden und den schottischen Athen den Ruf des Rationalismus und der Freisinnigkeit erwarben. Aber den im „Sartor Resartus" dem Professor Teufelsdröckh in den Mund gelegten Aeußerungen zufolge ließen auch diese Studien, wie das ganze Universitätsleben überhaupt, seine Höchsten dürstende Seele unbefriedigt. „Die hungerigen Jungen", sagt er, „blickten zu ihren geistigen Pflegern empor und statt Nahrung bot man ihnen unfruchtbaren Ostwind. Den leeren Jargon polemischer Metaphysik, Etymologie und mechanischer Manipulation, fälschlich Wissenschaft genannt, der dort im Schwange war, lernte ich freilich, besser vielleicht als die meisten andern. Unter elfhundert christlichen Jünglingen wird es nicht an elfen fehlen,

A page of Althaus's biography with Carlyle's annotations. *Courtesy of the National Library of Scotland, Edinburgh.*

One of the inserted sheets in which Carlyle describes *Sartor Resartus*. *Courtesy of the National Library of Scotland, Edinburgh.*

Oliver Cromwell: early copy of a painting by Sir Peter Lely. *Courtesy of Sidney Sussex College, Cambridge.*

Adam Skirving: oil by Archibald Skirving. *Courtesy of the Scottish National Portrait Gallery, Edinburgh.*

Index

Note. Numbers in italics designate references of particular importance.

INDEX